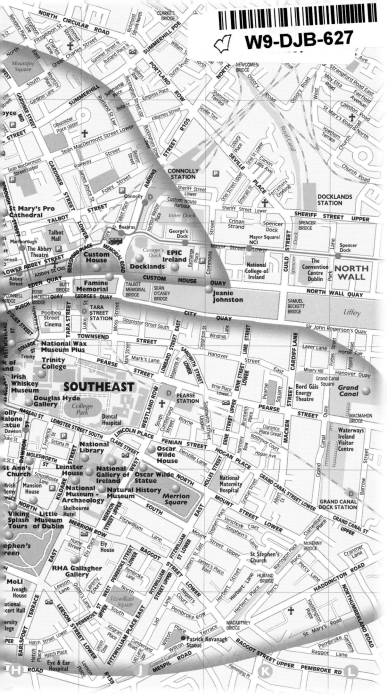

Fodor's
25 Best

DUBLIN

How to Use
This Book

KEY TO SYMBOLS	
✚ Map reference to the accompanying fold-out map	🛳 Nearest riverboat or ferry stop
✉ Address	♿ Facilities for visitors with disabilities
☎ Telephone number	❓ Other practical information
🕐 Opening/closing times	▷ Further information
🍴 Restaurant or café	ℹ Tourist information
🚆 Nearest rail station	✋ Admission charges: Expensive (over €8), Moderate (€3–€8) and Inexpensive (€3 or less)
Ⓜ Nearest subway (Metro) station	
🚌 Nearest bus route	

This guide is divided into four sections
● Essential Dublin: An introduction to the city and tips on making the most of your stay.
● Dublin by Area: We've broken the city into four areas, and recommended the best sights, shops, entertainment venues, nightlife and places to eat in each one. Suggested walks help you to explore on foot.
● Where to Stay: The best hotels, whether you're looking for luxury, budget or something in between.
● Need to Know: The info you need to make your trip run smoothly, including getting about by public transportation, weather tips, emergency phone numbers and useful websites.

Navigation In the Dublin by Area chapter, we've given each area of the city its own color, which is also used on the locator maps throughout the book and the map on the inside front cover.

Maps The fold-out map with this book is a comprehensive street plan of Dublin. The grid on this fold-out map is the same as the grid on the locator maps within the book. We've given grid references within the book for each sight and listing.

Contents

Introducing Dublin

Building and renovation in Dublin continues at full speed. Recent years have seen an influx of global technology companies, and the city is more buzzing, youthful and cosmopolitan than ever, yet there is also history at every turn.

The economic boom of the 1990s saw an influx of artists, musicians, film-makers, chefs and designers attracted by tax concessions and inexpensive property. The world recession, from 2008, saw sky-high property values plummet and jobs disappear. The Luas tram system and the Port Tunnel are legacies of the high-spending years that have made travel in and around Dublin much easier. The spectacular Samuel Beckett Bridge has given the city a new landmark, and there are new bridges in the pipeline.

There's a buzz in the streets and the stylish restaurants and cafés, pubs and smart bars always seem busy. Shopping is as good as ever, and frequent sales make the merchandise, from designer fashion to traditional and modern crafts, even more tempting. Dublin's cultural scene thrives, with theater productions, concerts and big stars performing at music venues, including the state-of-the-art 14,000-seater 3Arena. Traditional Irish music remains a huge draw in the city's pubs.

Even though Dublin is one of the most expensive cities in the world in which to build, there has been a recent building boom—from design-led cultural centers to smart new apartments to house the city's influx of global IT workers. The innovative modern architecture of the rejuvenated Docklands has opened up exciting urban spaces. But the old city is still there, its Georgian buildings and squares never ceasing to delight. Museums and art galleries are packed with well-displayed treasures, there's history aplenty, and the people are as welcoming as their legendary charm promises. A visit to Dublin is a great experience.

THE SPIRE IN FIGURES

- At 120m (394ft), the O'Connell Street monument is one of the world's tallest.
- Constructed from reflective stainless steel, the top 12m (39ft) of the structure are illuminated.
- The Spire's official name is Monument of Light, although locals rarely call it that.
- Completed in 2003, the Spire replaces Nelson's Pillar which was blown up in 1966.

WHAT'S THE *CRAIC*?

When used in Ireland "What's the *craic*?" generally means, What's happening? What's the gossip? President Obama asked a hall full of students this question to great applause. In fact, although most visitors consider it an authentic Irish word, *craic* derived from a Scottish or northern English word, crack—and the meaning is much the same.

BEST KNOWN LOCALS

Dublin's sons and daughters include plenty of famous names from the worlds of art, literature and music, many of whom have become legends.

Actors: Gabriel Byrne, Colin Farrell, Saoirse Ronan and Aiden Gillen.

Musicians: Van Morrison, Thin Lizzy, Sinead O'Connor and U2.

Writers: Bram Stoker, Brendan Behan, Oscar Wilde and James Joyce.

FASHIONABLE DISTRICT

Dignitaries and celebrities often stay outside central Dublin. The fashionable area of Ballsbridge and Lansdowne Road, to the southeast, are near the Aviva Stadium (which host international rugby and football), the Royal Dublin Society's arena (RDS) and the embassy belt with its excellent restaurants and classy hotels. Dublin is quite compact, so it doesn't take long to reach these areas from the city.

A Short Stay in Dublin

DAY 1

Morning It wouldn't be a true trip to Ireland without acquainting yourself with the black stuff and an early start at the **Guinness Storehouse** (▷ 30–31) will help you beat the crowds. You can get a bus down to St. James's Gate and spend a couple of hours touring the displays.

Late morning Take your free pint of Guinness or a coffee at the newly extended Gravity Bar at the top of the Storehouse, and you will be rewarded with great views of the city. Catch a bus or walk back to visit **Christ Church Cathedral** (▷ 25), or a trip around the adjoining **Dublinia** (▷ 28–29) for an excellent insight into the medieval life of the city.

Lunch Walk from the cathedral down Lord Edward Street into Dame Street. Just opposite **Dublin Castle** (▷ 26–27) you will find a quaint tea shop, the **Queen of Tarts** (▷ 44), where you can get an excellent light lunch. Afterward, visit the castle or the **Chester Beatty Library** (▷ 24), which has a rare collection of priceless books and Oriental art.

Afternoon Continue to the bottom of Dame Street, taking a left turn into Anglesea Street. Carry on until you come to the quay, and take a left and go first right over the **Ha'penny Bridge** (▷ 34), for good views of the River Liffey. Turn right onto the Liffey Boardwalk until you reach O'Connell Street, a busy road with shops, theaters, and landmarks such as the GPO and many statues.

Dinner Cross back over the river on O'Connell Bridge and toward Fade Street or Drury Lane, with its choice of stylish, cosmopolitan restaurants.

Late evening Nearby, have a pint in the traditional pub The Long Hall (▷ 40), or a glass of wine in The Wine Cellar (▷ 41).

DAY 2

Morning *The Book of Kells* in **Trinity College** (▷ 72–73) is tremendously popular, so head there when the library opens at 9.30am. Afterward, take a walking tour of the college grounds, led by a guide.

Late morning Walk to the front of the college and into Dublin's premier shopping street, Grafton Street, lined by high street names and designer shops. Stop for a coffee at the famous **Bewley's Café** (▷ 84–85). At the bottom of Grafton Street is **St. Stephen's Green Centre** (▷ 80–81), and **St. Stephen's Green** (▷ 70–71) with its lakes and lawns.

Lunch If the weather is nice have a picnic in the park. Alternatively, have a bite to eat in a nearby café on the north side of the green or walk to Dawson Street to enjoy lunch in one of its many restaurants.

Afternoon Take a stroll round the green, then take the exit to the north and cross over to Kildare Street. This is where you will find the city's grandest buildings, including the **National Museum – Archaeology** (▷ 69) with its many treasures, and the National Gallery. Continue round to **Merrion Square** (▷ 75) noting the blue plaques on buildings where famous former residents once lived, then inside the tiny park, to spot the wonderful reclining statue of **Oscar Wilde** (▷ 75–76).

Dinner Merrion Square has many of Dublin's top restaurants. Treat yourself at **Restaurant Patrick Guilbaud** (▷ 88) in the **Merrion Hotel** (▷ 112), the Michelin-starred **L'Ecrivain** (▷ 86) or classic Italian in the **Unicorn** (▷ 88).

Evening You can choose here from traditional pubs like **Doheny and Nesbitt** or the classy **Horseshoe Bar** at the Shelbourne Hotel (▷ 83).

ESSENTIAL DUBLIN A SHORT STAY IN DUBLIN

ESSENTIAL DUBLIN TOP 25

▶ ▶ ▶

Chester Beatty Library
▷ **24** Its galleries show off a rich collection of Oriental and religious objects.

Trinity College ▷ **72–73**
Ireland's premier seat of learning is home to one of the world's most beautiful medieval books.

Temple Bar ▷ **33**
Come here for cobbled streets, art and music museums, and a busy weekend market.

St. Stephen's Green
▷ **70–71** Take a break in Dublin's picturesque green space.

St. Patrick's Cathedral
▷ **32** Visit the embodiment of history and heritage of the Irish people.

Phoenix Park ▷ **96**
Vast green expanse with deer, Dublin Zoo and the Papal Cross.

**National Museum
– Decorative Arts &
History** ▷ **55** This barrack building houses furniture, weaponry and folk art.

Christ Church Cathedral
▷ **25** This has been the seat of Irish bishops since the time of Viking Dublin.

Dublin Castle ▷ **26–27**
Tour the hub of historic Dublin and the seat and symbol of secular power.

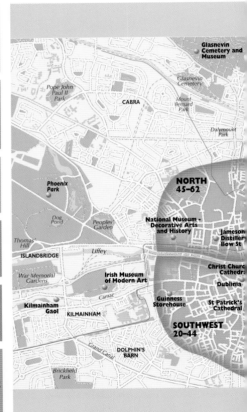

**National Museum –
Archaeology** ▷ **69**
See some of Ireland's prehistoric and Viking treasures.

National Gallery ▷ **68**
Ireland's foremost collection of art pays homage to the old masters.

**MoLI – Museum of
Literature Ireland** ▷ **67**
Displays over three floors showcase Ireland's writers.

These pages are a quick guide to the Top 25, which are described in more detail later. Here they are listed alphabetically, and the tinted background shows the area they are in.

Dublin City Gallery The Hugh Lane ▷ 48 Browse the Irish works alongside well-known paintings.

Dublin Writers Museum ▷ 49 A glowing tribute to the great literary figures of the city.

Dublinia ▷ 28–29 Relive life in Viking and medieval Dublin with this state-of-the-art exhibition.

EPIC Ireland ▷ 50–51 Interactive exhibits bring the Irish diaspora to life.

GAA Museum ▷ 92 Learn all about Ireland's sporting history and heroes at Croke Park.

Glasnevin Cemetery and Museum ▷ 93 This famous graveyard is a real Who's Who of Ireland.

GPO Museum Witness History ▷ 52 Exhibition about the events of the Easter Uprising.

Guinness Storehouse ▷ 30–31 Celebrate 250 years of the black stuff in a high-tech modern museum.

Irish Museum of Modern Art ▷ 94 Internationally acclaimed artists sit alongside local names.

James Joyce Centre ▷ 53 This cultural attraction is devoted to the great man of Irish literature.

The Little Museum of Dublin ▷ 66 A fascinating collection that documents 20th-century life in Dublin.

Kilmainham Gaol ▷ 95 This infamous jail gives a profound insight into Irish 19th and 20-century history.

Jameson Distillery Bow St. ▷ 54 Follow the making process of the famous Irish whiskey.

Map labels:
DRUMCONDRA
Griffith Park
MARINO
Tolka
Fairview Park
Royal Canal
Croke Park
HIBSBOROUGH
GAA Museum
EAST WALL
Dublin Writers Museum
James Joyce Centre
Dublin City Gallery The Hugh Lane
GPO Witness History
EPIC Ireland
NORTH WALL
Liffey
Temple Bar
Trinity College
RINGSEND
Dublin Castle
Chester Beatty Library
National Museum - Archaeology
National Gallery of Ireland
Merrion Square
Little Museum of Dublin
Dodder
MoLI
St Stephen's Green
Iveagh Gardens
Fitzwilliam Square
SOUTHEAST 63–88
RANELAGH
Grand Canal
BALLSBRIDGE

9

Shopping

The delight of shopping in bustling Dublin lies in the compact nature of the city and the fact that the best shopping areas are in close proximity. Top local designers and major fashion brands are represented, as are traditional stores and retro shops.

Variety Is the Key
What really makes shopping in Dublin so rewarding is the sheer variety of shops. Specialist shops tuck in alongside high street names, and home-grown talent blossoms amid international brands. Craftspeople merge the traditional with the modern, working in wood, silver, glass, ceramics, linen and wool to produce elegant up-to-the-minute designs. In Dublin you can find the best in beautifully made items, stylish home interiors and top-quality Irish food products.

Shopping Areas
Grafton Street, located south of the river, has always been the smartest shopping area in the city. With its street musicians and colorful flower stalls, there's always a buzz in this pedestrianized street lined with international and Irish fashion designer shops and chain stores, with the iconic Bewley's an essential coffee-stop along the way. Drury Street is seeing new independent boutiques, homeware stores and cafés popping up. Nearby, the Powerscourt Centre is the antidote to modern shopping malls. This fine 18th-century Georgian mansion is home to more than 40 specialty

KNOW YOUR *BODHRÁN* FROM YOUR BANJO

The *bodhrán* (pronounced "bough-rawn") is a simple and very old type of frame drum made of wood with animal skin—usually goat—stretched over the frame and decorated. It is played with a double-ended stick, rather than struck with the hands. Played for centuries in Ireland, it came onto the world stage in the 1960s with the rise of the Irish band The Chieftains. If you can't master the technique, try hanging it on your wall!

Clockwise from top left: Brown's store; Merrion Square; CHQ Building, Docklands;

boutiques as well as restaurants, bars and cafés. The Trinity College end of Grafton Street, Suffolk Street and Nassau Street are famed for their Irish design shops. Department stores and big, bright and airy shopping centers lie north of the river, on O'Connell Street and Henry Street. With plenty of parking, this revitalized area is popular with Dubliners.

Irish Products

Sample bohemian South Great George's Street, filled with second-hand, retro and ethnic stores. Explore Temple Bar's cobbled winding streets for unusual finds and Saturday markets. Francis Street is Dublin's antiques quarter, home to wonderful Irish furniture and silverware. Shop for Aran knitwear—every sweater is unique— and Donegal tweed, Waterford, Tipperary and Galway crystal, Mosse pottery, Belleek porcelain, Orla Kiely bags and traditional, fine Irish linen. Jewelry has a special place in Dublin; look for the exquisite replicas of the Tara Brooch, Claddagh rings and Celtic knots, mixing modern design with age-old tradition, and the work of new young designers with creative flair, especially the independent stores in Cow's Lane. In home interior shops you'll find contemporary designs based on time-honored patterns. Dublin is also the place to buy traditional musical instruments. Kitsch—much of it is mass-produced in Asia—is evident; examples of leprechauns, shamrocks and shillelaghs can be found in profusion in mainstream souvenir shops such as Carrolls.

LOCAL DELICACIES

Breads, farmhouse cheeses and smoked salmon are a few of the local delights, along with handmade creamy chocolates and truffles, some of them flavored with whiskey—try Butler's stores. The Saturday market in Meeting House Square is a great place to buy these products as are food stores such as Fallon & Byrne and Dollard & Co. Also look out for Guinness-flavored toffees and Irish Porter cake.

Powerscourt Townhouse; traditional pub in Temple Bar; fashionable Grafton Street

Shopping by Theme

Whether you're looking for a department store, a quirky boutique, or something in between, you'll find it all in Dublin. On this page shops are listed by theme. For a more detailed write-up, see the individual listings in Dublin by Area.

From cocktail bars and traditional pubs to live entertainment, Dublin boasts plenty of options. The city is famed for its theaters (it currently boasts 27) which reflects the city's great literary heritage. Big-name stars and hit musicals pack the massive 3Arena, while smaller venues feature a wide repertoire of plays, opera and concerts.

Anyone for a Drink?

Dublin pubs are an institution and a visit to a traditional bar to sample a pint of expertly poured Guinness or Murphy's stout should be part of your visit. Hip bars specialize in bespoke cocktails. Enjoy an evening of traditional Irish music; some venues hold live sessions nightly, mostly free (check for leaflets). Most bars close around 11.30pm or 12.30am, with many opening later at weekends (Fri and Sat night). There is a smoking ban at all indoor venues, and ID may be required if you're lucky enough to look under 18.

Have a Laugh

Expanding fast, Dublin's comedy scene sees plenty of new talent emerging. There is stand-up comedy at many pubs a couple of nights a week and, at other venues, comedians and other acts battle it out at open-mic nights to be acclaimed as that night's best act. The long-established Comedy Cellar at the International Bar on Wicklow Street hosts well-known local and international comedians, and is also known for attracting rising stars. The Laughter Lounge stages more established Irish names.

Cheers in Irish is sláinte. *Have a traditional night out in a pub or go to one of Dublin's historic theaters*

MERRION SQUARE

Evening light is kind to Dublin's Georgian architecture. Lit by street lamps, the imposing buildings and elegant squares resemble the set of a magnificent period drama. Take an evening stroll around Merrion Square, down Merrion Street Upper and on to Baggot Street to see the dramatic sight of the illuminated National Museum and the Government Buildings.

Where to Eat

Restaurants and bars continue to open at a bewildering rate, many of an excellent standard. Young, talented Irish chefs have transformed Dublin's menus, placing great emphasis on local ingredients, and the number of Michelin stars has grown. It's not all about top-class gourmet; there are plenty of cool coffee shops, vegan restaurants and independent bistros with global cuisine.

What's on Offer?
Look for good-value lunch specials and pre-theater menus (usually served before 7pm), when even upscale restaurants can become affordable. While the choice of dishes may be smaller at lunchtime, there's no dip in quality. The vast array of restaurants reflects Dublin's cosmopolitan character, from Mediterranean and European cuisines through to Thai, Japanese, Chinese, Malaysian and Middle Eastern specialties. There is a growing number of small, independent cafés serving good food—in addition to brewing excellent single-origin coffee, which is all the rage in Dublin.

Irish Cooking
Innovative chefs are taking the country's best, fresh ingredients and creating light, modern dishes full of taste that are then stylishly presented—transforming "traditional" Irish cuisine into something much more exciting. Organic and locally sourced seafood and meat are especially worth seeking out. With vegetarian food becoming more popular, you'll also find meat-free options in most restaurants.

Mealtimes
Breakfast may be served from 7am until 10am and lunch from 12 until 2.30pm, but with so many cafés, bistros and pubs open all day, finding something to eat is not a problem. Dinner is often served from around 5.30pm in restaurants, and last orders for food can be at 10pm. Many ethnic restaurants keep later hours.

There is so much on offer in Dublin, from oyster bars and historic cafés to stylish restaurants

Where to Eat by Cuisine

There are places to eat to suit all tastes and budgets in Dublin. On this page they are listed by cuisine. For a more detailed description of each restaurant, see Dublin by Area.

Asian
Chili Club (▷ 85)
Diep Le Shaker (▷ 85)
Langkawi (▷ 87)
Mongolian Barbeque (▷ 43)
Monty's of Katmandu (▷ 43)
Neon (▷ 43)
Pickle (▷ 43)
Saba (▷ 88)
Taste by Dylan McGrath (▷ 44)
Thai Orchid (▷ 44)
Yamamori (▷ 62)

Cafés
3Fe (▷ 84)
Bewley's Café (▷ 84)
Bread 41 (▷ 85)
Café Notto (▷ 41)
The Fumbally (▷ 42)
Lemon Crepe & Coffee Co (▷ 43)
One Society (▷ 62)
Science Gallery Café (▷ 88)
Queen of Tarts (▷ 44)

European
Bang Restaurant (▷ 84)
Le Bon Crubeen (▷ 61)
Dax (▷ 85)
Drury Buildings (▷ 42)
Dunne & Crescenzi (▷ 85)
Fade Street Social (▷ 42)
Fire (▷ 86)
The Greenhouse (▷ 86)

The Ivy (▷ 86)
MV Cill Airne (▷ 62)
Osteria Lucio (▷ 87)
La Peniche (▷ 87)
Restaurant Patrick Guilbaud (▷ 88)
Salamanca (▷ 44)
Toscana (▷ 106)
Trocadero (▷ 44)
The Unicorn Restaurant (▷ 88)
Uno Mas (▷ 44)

International
777 (▷ 41)
Avoca Salt (▷ 106)
Cornucopia (▷ 85)
Elephant and Castle (▷ 42
The Gotham Café (▷ 86)
Govinda's (▷ 42)
Wild Restaurant (▷ 88)

Markets
Eatyard (▷ 42)

Modern Irish
Le Bon Crubeen (▷ 61)
Chapter One (▷ 61)
Cleaver East (▷ 42)
L'Ecrivain (▷ 86)
Ely Bar & Grill (▷ 61)
Pichet (▷ 43)
The Pig's Ear (▷ 87)
The Saddle Room (▷ 88)
Variety Jones (▷ 44)
The Woollen Mills (▷ 62)

Seafood
Aqua (▷ 106)
Beshoff's (▷ 61)
Cavistons (▷ 106)
Fish Shop (▷ 62)
King Sitric (▷ 106)
Leo Burdock (▷ 43)

Steakhouses
Marco Pierre White Steakhouse & Grill (▷ 87)
Shanahan's on the Green (▷ 88)

Traditional Irish
Gallaghers Boxty House (▷ 42)
Hartley's (▷ 106)
Hatch & Sons Irish Kitchen (▷ 86)
L. Mulligan Grocer (▷ 62)
Pearl Brasserie (▷ 87)
The Winding Stair (▷ 62)

Turkish and Middle Eastern
Brother Hubbard (▷ 61)
The Cedar Tree (▷ 41)

Vegan
Veginity (▷ 62)

Top Tips For...

These great suggestions will help you tailor your ideal visit to Dublin, no matter how you choose to spend your time. Each suggestion has a fuller write-up elsewhere in the book.

BEST IRISH STYLE
Brown Thomas (▷ 78) showcases new and established Irish designers.
Avoca (▷ 78), a huge store, full of all things Irish, from homeware to clothing, plus a food hall with tasty delights.
The Design Tower (▷ 79) has jewelry, crafts and sculpture by local artists.

COOL CAFÉS
Sip an afternoon Americano at Bewley's (▷ 84), the iconic coffee house with its own blends.
Settle down at One Society (▷ 62), a cozy farm-to-table café.
Be tempted by cakes at Queen of Tarts (▷ 44), a local favorite for weekend brunch or afternoon tea.

SEAFOOD TREATS
Head out to classy Cavistons in coastal Dun Laoghaire (▷ 106).
DART out to Howth and treat yourself to the freshest of fish at the King Sitric restaurant (▷ 106).
Down-to-earth fish and chips are at their best eaten straight out of the fryer from Leo Burdock's takeout (▷ 43).
Taste local seafood classics at the tiny and unassuming restaurant, Fish Shop (▷ 62).

GOING MEAT FREE
For vegetarian and vegan dishes, head to Cornucopia. It's great for lunch (▷ 85).
Indian and veggie dishes at budget-friendly prices abound at Govinda's (▷ 42).
Veginity caters to a plant-based demand, with eclectic, globally inspired dishes (▷ 62).

Clockwise from top left: Avoca, Suffolk Street; Buswells hotel; enjoy a night out with cocktails and music; Viking Exhibition,

STAYING AT A GEORGIAN TOWNHOUSE

Four townhouses in one, the Merrion (▷ 112) remains one of Dublin's most luxurious hotels—period elegance at its best.

Savor Georgian charm at the friendly Buswells hotel (▷ 110) in leafy Dublin 4.

Relax at Stauntons on the Green (▷ 111), a calm oasis with a garden in the heart of the city.

Treat yourself at Number 31 (▷ 111), a period townhouse with 21st-century style.

SPORTING DUBLIN

Watch Gaelic football at Croke Park (▷ 104), Ireland's largest sporting venue and the headquarters for Ireland's traditional games for more than a century.

Go to at Tallaght Stadium (▷ 105) to cheer on Shamrock Rovers soccer team.

Join sports fans in The Bleeding Horse pub (▷ 82) to watch international rugby and soccer matches.

Watch student teams compete on Trinity College (▷ 72–73) sports fields.

TRADITIONAL MUSIC

Listen to Irish music every night at the Temple Bar pub The Merchants Arch (▷ 40).

For impromptu music visit O'Donoghue's (▷ 83), one-time haunt of the popular Irish band the Dubliners.

The Cobblestone (▷ 60), north of the river, has a regular program of Irish, blues and folk—check out the back room also.

Putting on nightly traditional music, The Brazen Head (▷ 39) is Dublin's oldest pub.

Dublinia; Dublin Zoo within Phoenix Park; Patrick Guilbaud restaurant

THINGS FOR KIDS

Dublin Zoo (▷ 96) is home to many and varied, impressive wild beasts.

Take to the water on a Viking Splash tour (▷ 76).

Thrill and enthrall them at the National Wax Museum Plus (▷ 35).

Explore Viking Dublin at the entertaining Dublinia (▷ 28–29).

A BUDGET-SAVVY TRIP

Make the most of free admission to the National Gallery (▷ 68) and the National Museum – Archaeology (▷ 69).

Explore the parks or Georgian squares, such as Merrion Square (▷ 75) and Phoenix Park (▷ 96)—they're free.

Pack a picnic and head for St. Stephen's Green (▷ 70–71), where sunny days bring Dubliners out for an alfresco lunch.

Take advantage of pre-theater menus at top restaurants for early evening fine-dining.

LUXURY

Be pampered at the Marker Hotel (▷ 112), with its gorgeous spa.

Dine at Ireland's leading French restaurant, Patrick Guilbaud (▷ 88).

Shop at Louise Kennedy (▷ 80) on Merrion Square for beautiful clothes and gifts.

Indulge in cocktails at Peruke & Periwig (▷ 84), in decadent surroundings.

THE GREAT OUTDOORS

Hire a bike in vast Phoenix Park (▷ 96–97) or stroll the lesser-known, peaceful Iveagh Gardens (▷ 74).

Take a trip on the DART (▷ 100–101) for a bracing walk along Howth's Head.

Play a round of golf—the choice of courses is huge (▷ 105).

Try your hand at stand-up paddleboarding at Grand Canal docks (▷ 74).

LITERARY GREATS

Find out about the city's famous scribes at the Dublin Writers Museum (▷ 49).

James Joyce is synonymous with Dublin—get an insight into the great man at the James Joyce Centre (▷ 53).

Oscar Wilde reclines languidly on a rock in Merrion Square, and his former home (▷ 75) is on the corner.

At the National Library (▷ 75), attend a temporary exhibition related to Ireland's writers.

From top: Enjoy live music and shopping; gardens at Merrion Square; James Joyce statue, Earl Street

Dublin by Area

The Southwest

The southwest area is one of the most historically interesting districts of the city. From the early Celtic and Viking settlements rose the medieval walled city of Dublin.

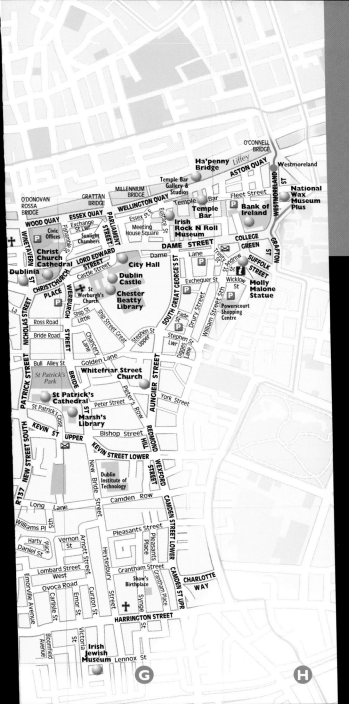

O'CONNELL
BRIDGE

Westmoreland

Ha'penny Bridge *Liffey*

ASTON QUAY

Temple Bar Gallery & Studios

MILLENNIUM BRIDGE

WELLINGTON QUAY

Fleet Street

WESTMORELAND ST

National Wax Museum Plus

GRATTAN BRIDGE

O'DONOVAN ROSSA BRIDGE

ESSEX QUAY

Temple Bar

Temple Bar

Bank of Ireland

WOOD QUAY

Civic Offices

Exchange St LWR

Fishamble St

Sunlight Chambers

Essex St E

Meeting House Square

Eustace St

Irish Rock N Roll Museum

COLLEGE GREEN

GRAFTON ST

Christ Church Cathedral

WINETAVERN ST

LORD EDWARD STREET

PARLIAMENT STREET

DAME STREET

Dame Lane

St Andrew St

SUFFOLK STREET

Dublinia

CHRISTCHURCH PLACE

Castle Street

City Hall

SOUTH GREAT GEORGE'S ST

Trinity St

Molly Malone Statue

Exchequer St

WERBURGH ST

St Werburgh's Church

Dublin Castle

Drury Street

Wicklow St

Chester Beatty Library

Ship St Little

Ship Street Great

Fade St

William Street Sth

Powerscourt Shopping Centre

NICHOLAS STREET

Ross Road

Bride Road

Chancery Lane

Stephen St Upper

Stephen St Lwr

Diggs Lane

La

Bull Alley St

Golden Lane

BRIDE STREET

Whitefriar Street Church

AUNGIER STREET

PATRICK STREET

St Patrick's Park

York Street

St Patrick's Cathedral

Peter's Row

Peter Street

REDMOND HILL

St Patrick's Close

Marsh's Library

Bishop Street

KEVIN ST UPPER

NEW STREET SOUTH

KEVIN STREET LOWER

New Bride Street

WEXFORD STREET

Dublin Institute of Technology

R137

Camden Row

CAMDEN STREET LOWER

Long Lane

Williams Pl

Pleasants Street

Pleasants Place

Harty Place

Vernon St

Daniel St

Arnott Street

Heytesbury

Grantham Street

CAMDEN ST UPR

CHARLOTTE WAY

Lombard Street West

Ovoca Road

Shaw's Birthplace

Grantham Place

Carlisle St

Emor St

Curzon Street

Synge Street

Emorville Avenue

HARRINGTON STREET

Bloomfield Avenue

Victoria St

Irish Jewish Museum

Lennox St

G

H

Chester Beatty Library

Historic treasures are displayed within the library's modern walls

THE BASICS

cbl.ie

✚ G7

✉ Dublin Castle

☎ 407 0750

🕐 Mon–Fri 10–5 (closed Mon Nov–Feb), Sat 11–5, Sun 1–5

🍴 Café

🚇 Tara Street

🚌 Cross-city buses

♿ Good

🎟 Free

❓ Audio-visual presentations. Free guided tours. Roof Garden

HIGHLIGHTS

● New Testament papyri
● Qu'ran manuscripts
● Persian and Mughal paintings
● Jade snuff bottles
● Silk Road Café

American-born Sir Alfred Chester Beatty is one of the few people to have been made an honorary citizen of Ireland, a gesture made in gratitude for the rare and priceless art collection that he bequeathed to the nation in 1956.

Hidden treasure The library and oriental art gallery named after its founder and benefactor, Sir Alfred Chester Beatty (1875–1968), is one of Dublin's jewels but is often overlooked. The unique collection is displayed on two floors in a converted Georgian building.

Masterpieces Alfred Chester Beatty, a very success-ful mining engineer born in New York and knighted for his services to Britain as an advisor to Winston Churchill during World War II, devoted much of his life to the search for manuscripts and objets d'art of the highest quality. Permanent exhibitions focus on two themes: Arts of the Book and Sacred Traditions. The library also stages temporary exhibitions. The collections range from c2700BC up to the present day, and stretch geographically from Japan to Europe. Religious writings range from one of the earliest known New Testament papyri to copies of the Qu'ran, all masterpieces of calligraphy. There is a wealth of Persian and Mughal miniature paintings as well as wonders of the East such as Burmese and Siamese painted fairy-tale books or *parabaiks*, Chinese silk paintings and jade snuff bottles, and Japanese *netsuke* and woodblock prints.

Christ Church Cathedral

The superb nave (left); majestic Christ Church Cathedral (right)

Christ Church Cathedral is not only one of Dublin's oldest stone buildings but it is an outstanding example of Norman architecture. It reflects 1,000 years of worship in Ireland.

History The older of Dublin's two cathedrals, Christ Church was founded by the Norse king Sitric Silkenbeard in 1038. The northern side of the choir and the south transept are the oldest parts of the existing stone structure and have been dated to just before 1180. This indicates that work started on it shortly after the Normans took over the city, employing masons brought over from England. The early Gothic nave, dated c1226–36, also reflects English taste. Its vault collapsed in 1562, leaving the north wall with an outward lean of about 45cm (18in).

Restoration Dublin whiskey distiller Henry Roe saved the building from ruin and paid for its reconstruction between 1871 and 1878. Flying buttresses were added to keep the whole edifice standing. Look for the effigy of a knight in armor near the entrance. It represents Strongbow, leader of the Anglo-Normans, who captured Dublin in 1170 and was buried in the cathedral in 1176. Head down to the original crypt, extending the entire length of the cathedral and housing the Treasury. Exhibits include valuable silver, the famous mummified cat and rat, mentioned by Joyce in *Finnegans Wake*, and the Heart of St Laurence O'Toole, stolen then returned to church in 2018.

THE BASICS

christchurchdcathedral.ie
- F7
- Christchurch Place
- 677 8099
- Apr–Sep Mon–Sat 9.30–7, Sun 12.30–3.15, 4.30–7; Mar and Oct Mon–Sat 9.30–6, Sun 12.30–3.15, 4.30–6; Nov–Feb Mon–Sat 9.30–5, Sun 12.30–3.15. Last admission 45 mins earlier.
- 49A, 50, 51B, 54A, 65, 77, 123
- Good
- Moderate

HIGHLIGHTS

- 12th-century south transept
- Leaning north wall
- Knight's effigy
- Crypt and "Treasures of Christ Church"
- Mummified cat and rat

Dublin Castle

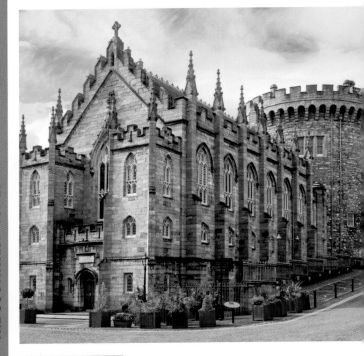

How many buildings in Europe can claim to have been the hub of a country's secular power for longer than Dublin Castle? It was the headquarters of English rule in Ireland for more than 700 years.

Ancient site Dublin Castle is now used for State occasions and presidential inaugurations, but it actually stands on the site of a much older Viking settlement. The castle occupies the southeastern corner of the Norman walled town overlooking the long-vanished black pool or *dubh linn* that gave the city its ancient Irish name. Lying below the castle the excavated remains of one of its circular bastions, the 13th-century Powder Tower, are clearly visible (although they are not accessible) on the guided tour.

Clockwise from far left: Stone exterior of the Chapel Royale; the castle's atmospheric red drawing room; a fountain in the castle grounds; the impressive throne room; Courtyard at Castle Hall

Interior After a fire in 1684, the interior was almost entirely rebuilt in the 18th and early 19th centuries. On the south side of Upper Castle Yard are the lavish State Apartments, where the English king's viceroy lived until the castle was handed over to the Irish State in 1922. It is known for its vast collection of decorative art, including Gandolfi's seven mythological paintings, plus rococo plasterwork ceilings and magnificent Waterford Crystal chandeliers. These regal rooms form the second half of the guided tour, which starts in the Powder Tower. The Gothic Chapel Royal is famed for its carved stone heads, carved oak galleries and intricate stained-glass windows. As this is a government building, some areas within the castle are occassionally closed because of official functions.

THE BASICS

dublincastle.ie

✚ G7

✉ Dame Street

☎ 677 7129

🕐 Daily 9.45–5.45. State Apartments closed occasionally for functions

🍴 Café

🚇 Tara Street

🚌 Cross-city buses

♿ State Apartments: good. Powder Tower: none

💷 Expensive

❓ Gardens, open Mon–Fri, not part of tour

Dublinia

HIGHLIGHTS

- Re-creation of medieval Dublin
- Archeology
- Interactive re-created Medieval Fair
- Viking re-creations
- View from St. Michael's Tower

If you want to know what made Dublin's Viking and medieval ancestors tick, visit Dublinia with its Viking exhibitions and audio-visual and interactive displays.

Vivid re-creation Dublinia, as the town was first recorded on a map of c1540, is a vibrant re-creation of medieval Dublin life housed in the former Synod Hall. After the Vikings had re-established the city in this area during the 10th century, Hiberno-Norsemen and Normans occupied it from 1170 until the end of the Middle Ages—the time span covered by Dublinia. In the section on Viking Dublin, kids can try on Viking clothes, attempt to decipher the runic alphabet, see a Viking warship and visit a cramped, smoky Viking house to get a feeling of the lifestyle and conditions.

Clockwise from far left: Viking in traditional headgear; learn about life in medieval Dublin and meet the Vikings—but mind the stocks; the medieval village from above

Excavations More than 30 years of extensive excavations in the Dublinia area during the 1970s, especially around Wood Quay, have uncovered objects such as leatherwork, pottery, floor tiles, jewelry and ships' timbers, which are on view in the new Level 3 exhibition, The Past Today. An interesting audio-visual presentation of the city's history complements a series of life-size model tableaux that illustrate episodes from the past. Archeology comes to life with the locally found skeletal remains of a Viking warrior and a medieval woman, affectionately named Maggie. To complete your visit with views of the city and river, climb up the 96 steps of the 17th-century St. Michael's Tower, part of the original church that stood on the site and incorporated into the Synod Hall when it was built.

THE BASICS

dublinia.ie

➕ F7

✉ St. Michael's Hill, Christchurch

☎ 679 4611

🕐 Mar–Sep daily 10–6.30 (last admission 5.30); Oct–Feb daily 10–5.30 (last admission 4.30)

🚌 50, 51B, 78A

🍴 Café

♿ Dublinia only: good

💷 Expensive

❓ Bookable tours, daily 2.30. Wheelchair accessible

Guinness Storehouse

THE TASTING ROOMS

HIGHLIGHTS

● Pint glass atrium
● Brewing exhibition
● Transportation section
● Classic advertisements and memorabilia
● Rooftop view

TIPS

● The admission fee includes a complimentary pint of Guinness.
● Flagship shop sells a range of Guinness merchandise.

Think Dublin, think Guinness. For more than 250 years, the black stuff has been an integral part of the city's economy and history. The Guinness Storehouse celebrates that legacy.

What's in a glass? The light-filled Atrium—which is actually the world's largest pint glass—is a perfect introduction to this 1904 building. Journey up through its seven floors to follow the production process of the brew, with interactive displays of the four main ingredients—hops, barley, yeast and water—as well as a powerful indoor waterfall.

Mine's a pint Make your way through the brewery of the past, founded by Arthur Guinness in 1759. To bring the story alive,

Clockwise from left: The cobblestone road in front of the old buildings remains from the early 1900s; the superb 21st-century atrium; the Gravity Bar; entering the Tasting Rooms at Guinness Storehouse

old equipment doubles up as interactive experiences. The huge wooden barrels, hand-made by master coopers, would have been transported to some 150 countries. The World of Advertising recalls classic Guinness adverts from the past 80 years, from posters to TV and digital campaigns. In the tasting rooms, you'll learn the best way to enjoy Guinness from a connoisseur. Put that knowledge to good use with a free pint at the recently expanded Gravity Bar on the top floor. It has splendid views over Dublin.

The Storehouse is Ireland's most popular visitor attraction; mornings are the least busy. For an after-hours experience (Thursday to Saturday evenings), you can also sample some brand-new craft beers at the adjacent Guinness Open Gate Brewery (▷ 39).

THE BASICS

guinness-storehouse.com
🞦 D7
✉ St. James's Gate
☎ 408 4800
🕐 Jul–Aug daily 9.30–9; rest of year 9.30–7 (last admission 2 hours before closing)
🍴 Bars, cafes, restaurants
🚌 51B, 78A from Aston Quay; 123 from O'Connell Street; Luas St. James's
♿ Excellent
💷 Expensive
❓ Shop

St. Patrick's Cathedral

TOP 25

St. Patrick's Cathedral (left); intricate carving in St. Patrick's choirstalls (right)

THE BASICS

stpatrickscathedral.ie

✚ F8

✉ St. Patrick's Close

☎ 453 9472

🕐 Mar–Oct Mon–Fri
9.30–5, Sat 9–6, Sun
9–10.30, 12.45–2.30,
4.30–6; Nov–Feb Mon–Fri
9.30–5, Sat 9–5, Sun
9–10.30, 12.30–2.30.
Visiting restricted during
services

🚍 Cross-city buses

♿ Good

✋ Moderate

❓ Guided tour (free)

HIGHLIGHTS

● Swift's bust and epitaph
● Medieval brasses
● Memorial to O'Carolan
● Organ

"Here is laid the body of Jonathan Swift, Doctor of Divinity, Dean of this Cathedral Church, where fierce indignation can no longer rend the heart. Go traveller, and imitate, if you can, this earnest and dedicated champion of liberty."

Literary connections Jonathan Swift's epitaph is a fitting tribute to the personality most often associated with St. Patrick's Cathedral. The author of *Gulliver's Travels*, Swift was the cathedral's outspoken Dean from 1713 until his death in 1745. He and his beloved friend, Esther Johnson, are buried in the south aisle.

History Founded in 1191 near a sacred well where St. Patrick is said to have baptized pagans, Ireland's national cathedral was built in Early English Gothic style and completed by 1284. Like Christ Church (▷ 25), St. Patrick's was heavily restored in the 19th century, with funds from the Guinness family. The cathedral embodies the heritage of the Irish people and receives over 300,000 visitors every year.

Monuments Look for the tomb and effigy of the 17th-century adventurer Richard Boyle, Earl of Cork, and a memorial to the Irish bard and harpist Turlough O'Carolan (1670–1738). In the south choir aisle are two of Ireland's rare 16th-century monumental brasses. George Frederick Handel practiced on the cathedral's organ before the first public performance of his *Messiah* in Dublin in 1742.

Traditional music at
Oliver St. John Gogarty
(left); advertising the
black stuff (right)

Temple Bar

**The area known as Temple Bar lies
between Dame Street and the River
Liffey. It takes its name from the Anglo-
Irish aristocrat Sir William Temple, who
owned land here in the 17th century. In
Viking times it was the heart of the city.**

Early beginnings Business flourished in
Temple Bar from the early 17th century but the
area fell into decline in the early 20th century
and by the late 1980s it had been proposed
as the site for a new bus terminal. Objections
were vociferous and the city's "left bank" began
to take off.

Dublin's Cultural Quarter Today, the
pedestrian-friendly cobbled streets form a
vibrant cultural district and are a huge draw
for tourists with their mix of restaurants,
quirky independent shops (especially vintage
clothing), markets, pubs and bars. It is the
venue for artists' studios, galleries, theater and
music. Temple Bar's popularity has meant that
there has been unwanted unruly behavior at
times, and it still gets rowdy at weekends, but
during the day it is great fun to explore. Nearby
Cow's Lane, Dublin's oldest district, is the setting
for Designer Mart, featuring local designers,
held on Saturday.

Meeting House Square This square, with
retractable roof, is the focus for performance
art, the summer open-air cinema and the
wonderful Saturday market (▷ 38, panel).

THE BASICS

templebar.ie
✚ G7
🚆 Tara Street
🚌 Cross-city buses

HIGHLIGHTS

● Meeting House Square
● Pubs, shops and cafés
● Markets: food (every Sat
10–4.30, ▷ 38) in Meeting
House Square; books (Sat,
Sun 11–6) in Temple Bar
Square

THE SOUTHWEST TOP 25

More to See

BANK OF IRELAND

This imposing and curved Palladian building, whose foundations were laid in 1729, was the upper and lower house of the old Irish Parliament, the focus of Ireland's years of freedom in the late 18th century.

➕ H7 ✉ 2 College Green ☎ 661 5933 🕐 House of Lords: Mon–Fri 10–4 (when not in use; check board outside) 🚆 Tara Street 🚌 Cross-city buses 🚻 Few 🎫 Free 🎟 Tours of House of Lords Tue 10.30–12.30

CITY HALL

dublincity.ie
Next door to Dublin Castle is the neoclassical, 18th-century City Hall, dominated by its decorative domed ceiling with gilded paintwork. Head downstairs to the multimedia exhibition, "The Story of the Capital," tracing Dublin's evolution from Viking times to present day, with artifacts that include the ceremonial Great Mace of Dublin.

➕ G7 ✉ Dame Street ☎ 222 2910 🕐 Mon–Sat 10–5.15 🚌 Cross-city buses 🚻 Good 🎫 Free

HA'PENNY BRIDGE

One of Dublin's most iconic landmarks, this was Ireland's first cast-iron bridge when it opened in 1816. The city's oldest pedestrian bridge, it was named for the halfpenny toll once charged to pedestrians to cross—each way.

➕ G6 ✉ Wellington Quay to Bachelors Walk 🚌 Cross-city buses 🎫 Free

IRISH JEWISH MUSEUM

jewishmuseum.ie
Comprising two terraced houses built in the 1870s, the museum is dedicated to the history of Irish Jews from the mid-19th century to the present day. The small community achieved prominence in the city's art, academic and medical fields. Displays show local life and Jewish cultural heritage.

➕ G9 ✉ 3 Walworth Road, off Victoria Street ☎ 490 1857 🕐 Oct–Apr Sun only 10.30–2.30; May–Oct Sun-Tue, Thu 11–3 🚌 16, 16A, 19, 19A, 122 🚻 Few 🎫 Free

IRISH ROCK N ROLL MUSEUM

irishrocknrollmuseum.com
Experience Irish music history with this behind-the-scenes tour of a real-life rehearsal and recording studio. You can even record your own song. Outside, don't miss the striking Wall of Fame.

➕ G7 ✉ Curved Street, Temple Bar ☎ 635 1993 🕐 Daily 11–5.30 🚌 Cross-city buses 🎫 Expensive

MARSH'S LIBRARY

marshlibrary.ie
This perfectly preserved hidden gem has hardly changed since opening more than 300 years ago. In the long gallery the shelves are filled with precious books dating from the 15th to 18th centuries and covering a range of subjects and languages. At the end of the shelves are cages, where readers were once locked when browsing the valuable books.

➕ G8 ✉ St. Patrick's Close ☎ 454 3511 🕐 Mon, Wed–Fri 9.30–5; Sat 10–5 🚌 Cross-city buses 🎫 Inexpensive

MOLLY MALONE STATUE

This life-size bronze statue of Molly Malone with her wheelbarrow honors the fishmonger, who

inspired the famous song. Molly Malone is believed to have lived and worked in Dublin until her death in 1734. The statue was presented to the city in 1984, and was located on Lower Grafton Street, before being moved to her new home, outside St. Andrew's Church, in 2014.

➕ H7 ✉ Suffolk Street 🚉 Pearse 🚌 Cross-city buses

NATIONAL WAX MUSEUM PLUS

waxmuseumplus.ie

Step through Irish history and a scary Chamber of Horrors; see lifelike wax models of Irish actors, musicians and sporting legends; and even make your own film to upload online. There's also a science zone with interactive exhibits—great for kids.

➕ H6 ✉ Westmoreland Street ☎ 671 8373 🕐 Daily 10–10 (last entry 9pm) 🚉 Tara Street 🚌 Cross-city buses 💷 Expensive

ROE & CO DISTILLERY

roeandcowhiskey.com

At its peak in the 1800s there were almost 40 breweries and distilleries here in the Liberties area, a number that later plummeted. This new whiskey distillery in the former Guinness brewery offers a great hands-on experience as well as a tour of the distillery. In small groups, you're then guided to a "cocktail and flavor" workshop, ending up with a whiskey tasting in the distillery's Power House bar.

➕ E7 ✉ 92 James's Street ☎ 6435 999 🕐 11–7 (last admission 5pm) 🚌 123 💷 Expensive

TEELING WHISKEY DISTILLERY

teelingdistillery.com

When it opened in 2015, this was Dublin's first new whiskey distillery for more than 125 years. Its excellent tours explain the long history of whiskey in Ireland, demonstrate the distilling process and end with a tasting session in the bar. The shop sells a wide selection of Teeling products, including the 2019 award-winning single malt.

➕ F8 ✉ 13–17 Newmarket ☎ 531 0888 🕐 10–4 (last tour) 🚌 27, 56A, 77, 151 💷 Expensive 🎫 Tours

WHITEFRIAR STREET CHURCH

whitefriarstreetchurch.ie

This Carmelite church is known for its shrines—including one containing the relics of St. Valentine, (his feast day is, of course, on February 14). The altar holds the medieval oak carving Madonna and Child, known as "Our Lady of Dublin."

➕ G8 ✉ 56 Aungier Street ☎ 475 8821 🕐 Mon–Fri 7.30–6, Sat 7.30–7, Sun 7.30am–8pm. Mass daily 🚉 Pearse 🚌 Cross-city buses ♿ Good 💷 Free

VAULTS LIVE

vaults.live

With costumed actors, this new attraction is an entertaining 60-minute romp through Ireland's history. It includes prominent Irish characters such as Molly Malone, a Viking, and Bram Stoker, who act out a series of scenarios. It is amusing, if slightly kitsch.

➕ F7 ✉ The Schoolhouse, John's Lane West ☎ 541 1485 🕐 Thu and Sat 11–7, Fri and Sun 11–4.30 (last entry) 🚌 Cross-city buses 💷 Expensive

Walk Along the Quays

The English-born architect James Gandon (1743–1823) played an important role in the beautification of Dublin.

DISTANCE: 1.5km (1 mile) **ALLOW:** 45 minutes

START

GEORGE'S QUAY
🚇 J6 🚌 Cross-city buses

❶ Start at George's Quay and look across to the Custom House (▷ 56), a magnificent neoclassical building built by British architect James Gandon between 1781 and 1791.

❷ At O'Connell Bridge, glance left along Westmoreland Street to see the portico (c1784–89) that Gandon added to the Old Parliament House, now the Bank of Ireland (▷ 34).

❸ Continue upstream past the metal bridge, known as the Ha'penny Bridge, constructed in 1816. Carry on past the pedestrian Millennium Bridge.

❹ At the Grattan Bridge look south along Parliament Street to Thomas Cooley's imposing City Hall (▷ 34), the headquarters of Dublin Corporation since 1852.

END

CHRIST CHURCH CATHEDRAL
(▷ 25) 🚇 F7 🚌 Cross-city buses

❽ Turn left up Fishamble Street, thought to be Dublin's oldest street, and where Handel's *Messiah* was first performed in 1742. Walk up to Christ Church Cathedral (▷ 25).

❼ Continue past the Civic Offices on your left, where excavations unearthed a Viking site in the 1970s, until you reach Merchant's Quay. This was the site of the first Viking crossing of the River Liffey in the ninth century.

❻ Take a look also at the sea horse statues. Just beyond is Betty Maguire's Viking Longboat sculpture, and Michael Warren's 1997 Hull of the Viking Ship outside the Civic Offices on Wood Quay.

❺ City Hall was built in 1769 before Gandon arrived in Dublin.

Shopping

ARTICLE
articledublin.com

Located in Lord Powerscourt's former dressing room, this luxury homeware store sells tableware, fabrics, stationery and more. Items include pieces from top Irish designers.

➕ H7 ✉ Powerscourt Centre, 59 South William Street ☎ 679 9268 🚉 Pearse 🚌 Cross-city buses

CLADDAGH RECORDS
claddaghrecords.com

This longstanding specialist music shop is tucked away in Temple Bar. It sells CDs and DVDs, from the countrified sound of Irish dance bands to traditional and contemporary Irish folk. The staff know their stuff.

➕ G7 ✉ 2 Cecilia Street, Temple Lane ☎ 677 0262 🚉 Tara Street 🚌 Cross-city buses

DESIGN CENTRE
designcentre.ie

A boutique collection on the top floor of the Powerscourt Centre (▷ 38), this has fashion from renowned Irish and international designers. Look out for elaborate hats from the famous milliner Philip Treacy.

➕ H7 ✉ Powerscourt Centre, 59 South William Street ☎ 679 5718 🚉 Pearse 🚌 Cross-city buses

DESIGN LANE
designlane.ie

Buy clothing, ceramics, jewelry and homewares from this popular design collective (previously Cow's Lane Designer Studio). On Saturdays, visit the outdoor Designer Mart located in Cow's Lane.

➕ G7 ✉ Essex Street West, Temple Bar ☎ 679 8366 🚉 Tara Street 🚌 Cross-city buses

DOLLARD & CO
dollardandco.ie

On the ground floor of a 19th-century printing house, this food hall and market is a haven of Irish and international products. The interesting Deli serves food all day.

➕ G7 ✉ 2–5 Wellington Quay ☎ 616 9606 🚉 Luas Jervis 🚌 Cross-city buses

FALLON & BYRNE
fallonandbyrne.com

Foodies make a beeline for this huge food hall, with deli counters, cheeses, charcuterie and breads. There's a small coffee bar for fresh brews and cakes, and the Wine Cellar downstairs (▷ 41) is a good spot for lunch.

➕ G7 ✉ 11–17 Exchequer Street ☎ 472 1010 🚌 Cross-city buses

FLIP/HELTER SKELTER
One of several vintage clothes shops in Temple Bar, these adjacent shops have two floors of men's and women's retro gear, from biker jackets to jeans.

➕ G7 ✉ 4 Fownes Street Upper, Temple Bar ☎ 671 4299 🚉 Tara Street 🚌 Cross-city buses

GEORGE'S STREET ARCADE
georgesstreetarcade.ie

This covered, Victorian arcade, Ireland's oldest, has an eclectic array of shops and stalls. You'll find everything from vintage clothes at Retro and second-hand vinyl at Spindizzy Records to tempting cakes at Lolly & Cooks.

➕ G7 ✉ Between South Great George's Street and Drury Street 🚉 Pearse 🚌 Cross-city buses

THE HARLEQUIN
This store is loved for its classy vintage clothing and accessories, especially those

from the 1920s. Check out the vintage handbags, which are a house specialty.

🔲 G7 ✉ 13 Castle Market ☎ 671 0202
🚆 Pearse 🚌 Cross-city buses

INDUSTRY & CO

industryandco.com

This is not a conventional gift shop, but many of the items here make perfect presents. Choose from Irish as well as international designs, with everything from Scandi-inspired homeware to eco-leather bags.

🔲 G7 ✉ 41 Drury Street ☎ 613 9111
🚌 Cross-city buses

IRISH DESIGN SHOP

irishdesignshop.com

Local jewelers Clare Grennan and Laura Caffrey created this stylish array of Irish crafts by notable local designers, from colorful throws and carved wood pieces to handmade plant pots and silver jewelry.

🔲 H7 ✉ 41 Drury Street ☎ 679 8871
🚌 Cross-city buses

JAM ART FACTORY

jamartfactory.com

A tiny gallery displaying a cute and humorous collection of Dublin-themed prints, cards, posters and jewelry by local artists.

🔲 F7 ✉ 64–65 Patrick Street ☎ 616 5671
🚌 Cross-city buses

JOHN FARRINGTON ANTIQUES

johnfarringtonantiques.com

This small shop specializes in jewelry, with a selection of commissioned pieces incorporating antique precious gems. Choose from rings, bracelets, necklaces or even pick up a tiara.

🔲 G7 ✉ 32 Drury Street ☎ 679 1899
🚆 Pearse 🚌 Cross-city buses

MCCULLOUGH PIGOTT

mcculloughpigott.com

This highly respected store run by music professionals, has a huge collection of traditional Irish musical instruments and sheet music.

🔲 G7 ✉ 11 William Street ☎ 677 3138
🚆 Pearse 🚌 Cross-city buses

O'SULLIVAN ANTIQUES

osullivanantiques.com

This is an Aladdin's cave of exquisite items from years gone by, located on a street known for its antiques stores. It's crammed with a fantastic range of 19th-century Mahogany furniture, Irish gilt mirrors, painted ceramics, card tables and delicate glassware.

🔲 F7 ✉ 43–44 Francis Street ☎ 454 1143
🚌 78A, 123

POWERSCOURT CENTRE

powerscourtcentre.ie

A warren of boutiques, gift and craft stores, restaurants, beauty salons and art galleries in a Georgian town house that hosted parties in the 18th century. Check out Design Centre (▷ 37) on the top floor.

🔲 H7 ✉ 59 South William Street ☎ 679 4144 🚆 Pearse 🚌 Cross-city buses

SATURDAY MARKET

Temple Bar's lively weekly food market in Meeting House Square (Sat 10–4.30) sells a variety of produce ranging from Japanese sushi to Mexican burritos. Local Irish produce forms a key part of the market, and includes fresh breads, jams, yogurts and vegetables. Those with a sweeter tooth will enjoy the handmade fudge and chocolate or freshly cooked waffles and crêpes. There are cheeses, olives, oysters and more — depending on the day.

Entertainment and Nightlife

THE BAR WITH NO NAME
nonamebardublin.com
It may have no official name (look for the snail sign), but this bar does have a bunch of boho living rooms and a huge terrace. Open until 2.30am at weekends.
⊞ G7 ✉ 3 Fade Street ☎ 087 122 1064 (mobile) 🚌 Cross-city buses

BRAZEN HEAD
brazenhead.com
Reputedly the oldest bar in town—it has been trading since 1198—the Brazen Head has an old-world charm. It offers food in the afternoons and evenings, and traditional Irish music nightly.
⊞ F7 ✉ 20 Bridge Street Lower ☎ 679 5186 🚌 121

BUTTON FACTORY
buttonfactory.ie
This premier music venue with a 550 capacity holds themed club nights and live music. It also houses Crowbar, a more intimate music space and bar.
⊞ G7 ✉ Curved Street, Temple Bar ☎ 670 9105 🚊 Tara Street 🚌 Cross-city buses

FARRIER & DRAPER
farrieranddraper.ie
Spread over three floors, this quirky cocktail bar with walls crammed with paintings has colorful, mismatched armchairs. Open fires and deep couches give it a romantic feel, perfect for a classy cocktail or local craft beer.
⊞ H7 ✉ Powerscourt Town house, 59 South William Street ☎ 677 1220 🚌 Cross-city buses; Luas Dawson Street

THE GEORGE
thegeorge.ie
Dublin's best known and oldest LGBTQ+ bar, this place draws mixed crowds. Its main club venue is a lively space for regular events and theme nights—karaoke, drag acts and bingo nights.
⊞ G7 ✉ South Great George's Street ☎ 671 3298 🚌 Cross-city buses

GUINNESS OPEN GATE BREWERY
guinnessopengate.com
Taste rotating, experimental beers from St. James's Gate brewers. In the Taproom, part of the Guinness brewing lab and next to the fermenting tanks, casks and barrels, a €9 entry fee (Thu–Sat evening; book online) gives you a paddle of four 33cl exclusive tasters. It also serves pizza and mac 'n' cheese.
⊞ D7 ✉ St Thomas Street ☎ 471 2455 🚌 13, 40, 123; Luas James's

HOGAN'S
This lively bar is popular with Dublin's clubbing crowd, with DJ sets in the basement and weekend brunch in the bright main bar.
⊞ G7 ✉ 35 South Great George's Street ☎ 677 5904 🚌 Cross-city buses

IRISH FILM INSTITUTE
ifi.ie
An art-house cinema showing Irish independent and international films, the IFI has occasional free events and curated seasons. It also has an informal bar/restaurant, plus a shop.
⊞ G7 ✉ 6 Eustace Street, Temple Bar ☎ 679 5744 🚊 Tara Street 🚌 Cross-city buses

---

STAR TURN
When it comes to the live music scene, the city's major concert venues, such as the 3Arena and Olympia Theatre, feature top stars. Past acts include Robbie Williams, Adele and Cher. You will need to book well in advance.

THE LONG HALL

Time seems to have stood still in this traditional hostelry, with a long bar, smoked glass and ornate paintwork.
➕ G7 ✉ 51 South Great George's Street
☎ 475 1590 🚌 Cross-city buses

THE MARKET BAR

marketbar.ie
Tucked away at the back of George's Street Arcade (▷ 37), this spacious bar is named after the meat market that stood nearby. High ceilings, a tapas menu and a cool vibe—with no music—make it a grown-up place for a drink.
➕ G7 ✉ 14a Fade Street ☎ 613 9094
🚌 Cross-city buses

THE MERCHANTS ARCH

merchantsarch.ie
Enjoy traditional live music from several bands every night at this well regarded bar. Big screens show Ireland's live sports events and food is served all day.
➕ G7 ✉ 48–49 Wellington Quay ☎ 607 4010 🚌 Cross-city buses

OLYMPIA

olympia.ie
Dublin's oldest theater, most recently refurbished in 2016, attracts singers, musicians, stage shows, comedy acts and Christmas pantomimes onto its ornate stage.
➕ G7 ✉ 72 Dame Street ☎ 679 3323
🚉 Tara Street 🚌 Cross-city buses

PALACE BAR

thepalacebardublin.com
Established in 1843, this traditional pub still retains its old frosted glass and mahogany interior and was once a favorite of many literary giants.
➕ H6 ✉ 21 Fleet Street ☎ 671 7388
🚌 Cross-city buses

MOVIE FACTS

● IFI (▷ 39), the Savoy, the Light House and Cineworld Cinema are all venues for the Dublin International Film Festival (DIFF) in February/March.
● Tickets for the movies are usually cheaper during the day.
● New films are sometimes released earlier in Ireland than in the UK due to the film distribution system.
● On Saturday nights from June to September there are free showings of films at Meeting House Square in Temple Bar.

THE PORTERHOUSE

theporterhouse.ie
Dublin's first microbrewery is still doing an excellent job. It brews its own ales, stouts, three lagers and the specials on the premises, and stocks a huge range of bottled beers. Good food is served, and there's live music nightly.
➕ G7 ✉ 16–18 Parliament Street, Temple Bar
☎ 679 8847 🚌 Cross-city buses

PROJECT ARTS CENTRE

projectartscentre.ie
With visual arts to dance, music and theater, in two performance spaces and a gallery, this contemporary arts space gives Irish talent the chance to shine.
➕ G7 ✉ 39 East Essex Street ☎ 881 9613
🚉 Tara Street 🚌 Cross-city buses

SMOCK ALLEY THEATRE

smockalley.com
Dublin's first Theatre Royal opened on this site in 1662, closed in 1787, and reopened as a theater in 2012 after extensive renovation. It now stages contemporary drama, dance and occasional music festivals.
➕ G7 ✉ 6–7 Exchange Street Lower ☎ 677 0014 🚉 Pearse 🚌 Cross-city buses ❓ Tours

STAG'S HEAD

stagshead.ie

Built in 1770 and restyled in 1895, this traditional pub has ornate stained-glass windows, wood carvings and ironwork. Live music and hearty food.

🚩 G7 🖂 1 Dame Court ☎ 679 3687
🚉 Tara Street 🚌 Cross-city buses

WHELAN'S

whelanslive.com

With excellent acoustics and plenty of space many up-and-coming Irish groups and overseas bands headline here. Some of the 18th-century wood and stone features remain in its main bar, which opens late every night.

🚩 G8 🖂 25 Wexford Street ☎ 478 0766
🚉 Pearse 🚌 16, 16A, 19, 19A, 65, 83

THE WINE CELLAR

fallonandbyrne.com

The basement of Fallon & Byrne (▷ 37) is an informal venue with a good selection of wines for sale. Choose from any of the bottles, with low corkage, and order one of the sharing platters and mains from its food menu.

🚩 G7 🖂 11–17 Exchequer Street ☎ 472 1012 🚌 Cross-city buses

THE WORKMAN'S CLUB

theworkmansclub.com

This down-to-earth live music venue has different spaces, for a variety of musical genres, including Irish bands. There is also a regular program of DJ nights.

🚩 G7 🖂 10 Wellington Quay ☎ 670 6692
🚌 Cross-city buses

Where to Eat

777 (€€)

777.ie

This fun Mexican tapas restaurant and bar serves dishes such as chorizo and habanero, sea bream carpaccio and plenty of vegan dishes. The bar serves fabulous margaritas and other cocktails.

🚩 G7 🖂 7 Castle House, South Great George's Street ☎ 425 4052 ⏰ Mon–Sat dinner, Sun lunch, brunch and dinner
🚌 Cross-city buses

CAFFÉ NOTTO (€)

Occupying space in a former bank and in a handy location near Dublinia and Christ Church Cathedral, this is a great spot to relax with coffee, cake and sandwiches or sample the excellent soup with Irish soda bread.

🚩 F7 🖂 79 Thomas Street ☎ 454 7223
⏰ Mon–Fri 8–6, Sat and Sun 10–4
🚌 Cross-city buses

THE CEDAR TREE (€€)

Sample authentic Lebanese dishes and meze at this family-run restaurant decorated with a Middle Eastern theme. There is a decent selection of wines from the new and old worlds, plus some good Lebanese wines to choose from. For something different, there are

belly-dancing displays in the restaurant on Saturday evenings.

🔲 H7 ✉ 11 St. Andrew's Street ☎ 677 2121 🕐 Dinner only 🚉 Pearse 🚌 Cross-city buses

CLEAVER EAST (€€€)

cleavereast.ie

Irish chef Oliver Dunne has created a menu of sharing dishes and tasting plates celebrating local ingredients, such as crispy duck and teriyaki Atlantic halibut. It's situated inside the elegant Clarence Hotel.

🔲 G7 ✉ 6–8 Wellington Quay ☎ 531 3500 🕐 Lunch Fri–Sun, dinner daily 🚌 Cross-city buses

DRURY BUILDINGS (€€)

drurybuildings.com

This relaxed restaurant above the informal cocktail bar uses a Josper charcoal grill for exquisite dishes such as sea bass fillet and ribeye steak. Its tables overlooking the garden are sublime.

🔲 G7 ✉ 52–55 Drury Street ☎ 960 2095 🕐 Mon–Sat dinner 🚌 Cross-city buses

EATYARD (€)

the-eatyard.com

For inexpensive food on the go, this street food market has rotating cuisines and specialties, from Mexican dishes to free-range sausages and vegan "vish" and chips. Find a bench to eat at.

🔲 G9 ✉ 9–10 South Richmond Street 🕿 No phone 🕐 Thu–Sat noon–10, Sun noon–8 🚌 Cross-city buses

ELEPHANT AND CASTLE (€€)

elephantandcastle.ie

This popular place boasts one of Dublin's largest breakfast and brunch menus, including American and European favorites and full Irish breakfast. It gets busy, especially on Sundays.

🔲 G7 ✉ 18 Temple Bar ☎ 679 3121 🍴 Breakfast, brunch, lunch and dinner daily 🚉 Tara Street 🚌 Cross-city buses

FADE STREET SOCIAL (€€)

fadestreetsocial.com

On a small street packed with dining and nightlife spots, Dylan McGrath uses local produce to create interesting Irish and European dishes. Try braised rabbit in white wine or beef and Guinness stew with parsnip puree. The gastro bar offers a tapas menu.

🔲 G7 ✉ 6 Fade Street ☎ 604 0066 🕐 Lunch Tue–Sat, dinner daily; Gastro bar: tapas daily 5pm till late 🚌 Cross-city buses

THE FUMBALLY (€)

thefumbally.ie

A group of food-loving friends set up this informal café, popular for its coffee and mainly organic menu. Irish breakfast, Middle Eastern wraps, fresh soups and homemade cakes are on offer.

🔲 F8 ✉ Fumbally Lane ☎ 529 8732 🕐 Breakfast and lunch (till 5pm) Tue–Sat, dinner Wed 🚌 Cross-city buses

GALLAGHERS BOXTY HOUSE (€€)

boxtyhouse.ie

Come to this hugely popular, informal venue for traditional food focusing on the boxty, an Irish potato dish in the form of pancakes or dumplings.

🔲 G7 ✉ 20–21 Temple Bar ☎ 677 2762 🕐 Lunch and dinner daily 🚉 Tara Street 🚌 Cross-city buses

GOVINDA'S (€)

govindas.ie

Choose from a small selection of Indian dishes at this informal, simple café run by Hare Krishnas. It also serves European dishes, but the specialty paneer is recommended.

CELTIC COOKING

Today's Irish cooking draws inspiration from many sources, but simplicity is the key when it comes to serving fresh local produce. Smoked salmon, oysters, hearty soups and stews are readily available in most Dublin restaurants and pubs. Some adopt a traditional style, serving comfort food, such as seafood chowder and Irish stew, in settings with turf fires and local music, while others are culinary trend-setters nationally and internationally.

🔲 G7 ✉ 4 Aungier Street ☎ 475 0309
🕐 Lunch and dinner Mon–Sat 🚌 Cross-city buses

LEMON CREPE & COFFEE CO (€)

lemonco.com
Head here for mouthwatering savory and sweet crêpes and waffles, and wash them down with some great coffees.
🔲 G7 ✉ 66 South William Street ☎ 672 9044 🕐 Daily from 8am 🚆 Pearse
🚌 Cross-city buses

LEO BURDOCK (€)

leoburdock.com
This famous "chipper" has been serving takeout fish and chips since 1913. In addition to cod and haddock, it offers jumbo tiger prawns and battered sausage with thick-cut chips.
🔲 G7 ✉ 2 Werburgh Street ☎ 454 0306
🕐 Daily 🚌 Cross-city buses

MONGOLIAN BARBEQUE (€)

mongolianbbq.ie
Compile your own dish at this buffet of Asian ingredients. Your choice of meat, fish and vegetables, with sauces and spices, is cooked in front of you.
🔲 G7 ✉ 7 Anglesea Street ☎ 670 4154
🕐 Lunch and dinner daily 🚌 Cross-city buses

MONTY'S OF KATMANDU (€€)

montys.ie
The city's only Nepalese restaurant, with deep-red walls and dark wood, offers intriguing South Asian dishes, including Nepalese lamb masala and plenty of vegetarian side dishes.
🔲 G7 ✉ 28 Eustace Street ☎ 670 4911
🕐 Lunch Mon–Sat, dinner daily 🚆 Tara Street
🚌 Cross-city buses

NEON (€–€€)

neon17.ie
Neon offers an informal atmosphere and Asian street food. The Thai chefs create some real Southeast Asian favorites, like Singapore noodles, prawn *massaman* curry and *nasi goreng*. Dine at communal tables surrounded by urban-rustic decor.
🔲 G9 ✉ 17 Camden Street Lower ☎ 405 2222 🕐 Mon–Fri from 5pm, Sat–Sun from 2pm 🚌 Cross-city buses

PICHET (€€)

pichet.ie
Classic bistro food with fresh, seasonal ingredients, such as mussels and duck, is produced here by award-winning chef Stephen Gibson. Service is good and the interior is plush and spacious.
🔲 H7 ✉ 14–15 Trinity Street ☎ 677 1060
🕐 Daily lunch and dinner 🚆 Harcourt
🚌 Cross-city buses

PICKLE (€€)

picklerestaurant.com
Chef Sunil Ghai adapts his mother's traditional recipes in a smart new North Indian restaurant. Try the khatti fish curry or Rajasthani lamb shank, all beautifully presented.
🔲 G9 ✉ 43 Camden Street ☎ 555 7755
🕐 Wed–Fri lunch, Tues–Sun dinner 🚌 Cross-city buses; Luas Harcourt

QUEEN OF TARTS (€)

queenoftarts.ie

As its name suggests, you'll find tasty cakes, bakes and tarts, plus hot food for breakfast and lunch, all made on the premises at this tiny traditional tea shop. There is a bigger venue on nearby Cow's Lane. Note: it is very popular for weekend late breakfast.

G7 ✉ Cork Hill, Dame Street ☎ 670 7499 🕐 Daily breakfast, lunch (open till 7pm) 🚇 Tara Street 🚌 Cross-city buses

SALAMANCA (€€)

salamanca.ie

With deep red walls and chandeliers, Salamanca is a relaxed venue serving Spanish tapas. Start with some excellent Spanish olives, then opt for traditional paella or the range of dishes to share such as Serrano ham with manchego cheese and king prawns in white wine sauce. There are good value lunch and early bird menus.

H7 ✉ 1 St. Andrew's Street ☎ 677 4799 🕐 Lunch and dinner daily 🕐 Cross-city buses; Luas Dawson Street

TASTE BY DYLAN MCGRATH (€€€)

tasteatrustic.com

Executive chef McGrath creates divine dishes with Japanese, Spanish and South American influences in his stylishly contemporary restaurant. Try the five-course tasting menu, including sashimi, steak and green tea brulée.

H7 ✉ 17 South Great George's Street ☎ 526 7701 🕐 Wed–Sat dinner 🕐 Cross-city buses

THAI ORCHID (€€)

thaiorchiddublin.com

Spread over three floors, this restaurant serves all the established Thai specials, all freshly cooked and well presented. Courteous Thai staff in traditional costume serve, and Thai music plays softly in the background.

H6 ✉ 7 Westmoreland Street ☎ 671 9969 🕐 Lunch and dinner daily 🚌 Cross-city buses

TROCADERO (€€–€€€)

trocadero.ie

Going strong since 1957, this classic venue is still a favorite of well-heeled locals. It has a long tradition as a theater restaurant, with many photos on the wall of famous faces who have dined here. European and Irish dishes, such as roast rack of Wicklow lamb, use top local products. There's also a good pre-theater menu.

H7 ✉ 4 St. Andrew's Street ☎ 677 5545 🕐 Daily 4.30pm till late 🚌 Cross-city buses

UNO MAS (€€–€€€)

unomas.ie

At this simple, modern restaurant, expect food wth heavy Spanish influences. Some of the beautifully cooked dishes may include squid a la plancha and suckling pig.

G7 ✉ 6 Aungier Street ☎ 475 8538 🕐 Lunch Tue–Sat, dinner Mon–Sat 🚌 Cross-city buses

VARIETY JONES (€€–€€€)

varietyjones.ie

Don't be fooled by the unassuming appearance of this fabulous bistro—the tables get booked up weeks in advance. In 2019, less than a year after it opened, Variety Jones won a coveted Michelin star for Keelan Higgs' delightful, seasonal menus. Expect exquisitely cooked Irish dishes, such as trout with dill and yeast mousse.

F7 ✉ 78 Thomas Street ☎ 516 2470 🕐 Tue–Sat dinner 🕐 Cross-city buses

The North

The area north of the River Liffey is home to O'Connell Street and, off this famous thoroughfare, many of Dublin's smart shopping streets. The Docklands here are also developing rapidly.

Top 25

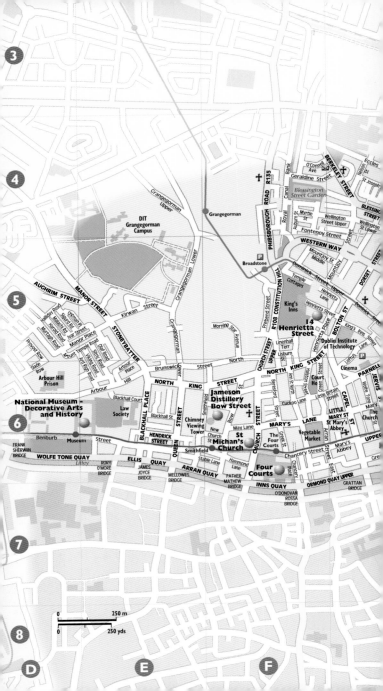

3

4

5

6

7

8

O'Connell Ave

Geraldine Street

BERKELEY STREET

Eccles
St Joseph

Canal Bank

R135

Blessington
Street Garden

Myrtle
St

Wellington
Street Upper

BLESSINGTON STREET

Wellington
St Lower

DORSET STREET

Fontenoy Street

WESTERN WAY

Mountjoy St
Middle

Dominick Street Upper

Temple
Cottages

Henrietta
Lane

PHIBSBOROUGH ROAD

Royal

GRANGEGORMAN UPPER

Grangegorman

**DIT
Grangegorman
Campus**

Broadstone

CONSTITUTION HILL

R108

Prebend Street

**King's
Inns**

Henrietta Street

**14
Henrietta
Street**

BOLTON ST

King's Inns Street

Dominick Street Lower

AUGHRIM STREET

MANOR STREET

Kirwan Street

GRANGEGORMAN LOWER

Morning Star Avenue

Linenhall
Terr

Lisburn
St

**Dublin Institute
of Technology**

Galway Road
Sligo Rd
Meath Rd

Osmond Rd
Villa Street
War Street

STONEYBATTER

North Brunswick

Street

Street

North

CHURCH STREET UPPER

Henrietta Street

NORTH KING STREET

Halliday Road
Murtagh Road
Merchant Road

Manor Place

Temple Cottages
Sitric Road

Olaf Road
Viking Road

North

KING

Smithfield

**Jameson
Distillery
Bow Street**

Court
Ho

Cinema

PARNELL

Wolfe Tone St

Little Britain St

JERVIS

Prospect Row
Slade Row

Mount
Temple Road
Arbour Hill Road

Arbour
Place

Arbour

Hill

STREET

STREET

Arbour

NORTH

Chimney
Viewing
Tower

Bow

St

Cuckoo Lane

MARY'S

LANE

**LITTLE
MARY ST**

Arran Street East

CAPEL ST

Mary's
The Church

**Arbour Hill
Prison**

**Law
Society**

Blackhall Court

PLACE

King

**New
Church**

May Lane

**St
Michan's
Church**

**The
Four
Courts**

**Vegetable
Market**

**Mary's
Abbey**

UPPER

**National Museum -
Decorative Arts
and History**

Blackhall St

BLACKHALL

**HENDRICK
STREET**

QUEEN

CHURCH STREET

**FRANK
SHERWIN
BRIDGE**

Benburb

Museum

Street

Smithfield

Stable Lane

Hammond Lane

Chancery Street

ORMOND QUAY UPPER

**GRATTAN
BRIDGE**

WOLFE TONE QUAY

Liffey

**RORY
O'MORE
BRIDGE**

**ELLIS
QUAY**

**JAMES
JOYCE
BRIDGE**

**MELLOWES
BRIDGE**

ARRAN QUAY

**FATHER
MATHEW
BRIDGE**

**Four
Courts**

INNS QUAY

**O'DONOVAN
ROSSA
BRIDGE**

Gre

0 ____ 250 m

0 ____ 250 yds

D

E

F

Mater Hospital
(Private)

Street

Temple
Street
Theatre

Temple
Street
Childrens
Hospital

North

Mountjoy
Square

WEST

SOUTH

SUMMERHILL

Belvedere
College

Dublin City Gallery
The Hugh Lane

James Joyce
Centre

Dublin Writers
Museum

PARNELL STREET

Gloucester
Place Upper

Garden of
Remembrance

The Gate
Rotunda
Hospital

Parnell
Statue

Sean MacDermott Street Lower

Sean MacDermott
Street Upper

CATHAL
BRUCHA
STREET

MARLBOROUGH STREET

GARDINER STREET

Railway

James Joyce St.

Foley Street

O'Connell Upper

Dominick

Cinema

St Mary's Pro
Cathedral

Cathedral
Street

TALBOT

Connolly

STREET

Busáras

AMIENS STREET KIOS

Theatre

Ilac
Shopping
Centre

The Spire

GPO Witness
History

James
Joyce
Statue

Marlborough

Talbot
Mall

EPIC
Ireland

Henry St.

Prince's St N

James
Joyce
GPO

LOWER ABBEY STREET

The Abbey
Theatre

Custom
House

MEMORIAL RD

Docklands

Jervis
Shopping
Centre

'vis

James Larkin Statue

O'Connell

Abbey St Old

CUSTOM

HOUSE QUAY

ABBEY STREET

MIDDLE ABBEY ST

Daniel
O'Connell
Statue

Abbey
Street

EDEN

QUAY

Famine
Memorial

BUTT
BRIDGE

TALBOT
MEMORIAL
BRIDGE

SEAN O'CASEY
BRIDGE

North Lotts

ROSIE
HACKETT
BRIDGE

Jeanie
Johnston

BACHELORS WALK

Liffey

rand Street

O'CONNELL
BRIDGE

O'CONNELL

RMOND QUAY LOWER

Ha'penny
Bridge

MILLENNIUM
BRIDGE

G · H · J

Dublin City Gallery
The Hugh Lane

Detail of Harry Clarke stained glass (left); the gallery's 18th-century exterior (right)

THE BASICS

hughlane.ie
⊞ G5
✉ Charlemont House,
Parnell Square North
☎ 222 5550
🕐 Tue–Thu 9.45–6, Fri
9.45–5, Sat 10–5, Sun 11–5
🍴 Café
🚃 Connolly
🚌 Cross-city buses
♿ Good
✋ Free

HIGHLIGHTS

● Impressionist paintings
● Stained glass by Harry
Clarke
● Francis Bacon Studio
● Free concerts on Sunday
Sep–Jun
● The Sean Scully Gallery

Degas, Monet and Renoir are among the Impressionist artists whose paintings are on display in this gallery which also looks back over 100 years of Irish art, including paintings and stained glass.

Philanthropist The Hugh Lane Gallery fills a niche between the old masters on display in the National Gallery (▷ 68) and the ultra-modern works in the Irish Museum of Modern Art (▷ 94). Built as a town house in 1763 by the Earl of Charlemont, the gallery now bears the name of Sir Hugh Lane, who drowned when the *Lusitania* sank in 1915. Before his death, Sir Hugh amended his will, stating that a group of 39 of his Impressionist pictures, which were then in London, should go to Dublin. However, the codicil was unwitnessed, so London kept the canvases until an agreement was reached in 1959 that the two cities would share the m. The gallery has a program of temporary exhibitions, including retrospectives of Irish abstract art in the Sean Scully gallery. Visit the perfectly reconstructed, chaotic London studio of Francis Bacon, complete with all its contents of more than 7,500 items.

Modern art Major Irish artists, including Osborne, Yeats, Orpen, Bacon and Le Brocquy, are well represented, and modern European artists include Beuys and Albers. There are also stained-glass pieces by Clarke, Hone and Scanlon.

The Gallery of Writers (left); a stained-glass tribute to Dublin's writers (right)

Dublin Writers Museum

Dublin has become the hub of a great literary tradition, and for centuries a meeting point for gifted writers. This museum celebrates their diverse talents and displays a fascinating mix of the writers' memorabilia.

Great Irish writers Many languages have been spoken by Ireland's inhabitants throughout the centuries, but it was the establishment of English in the 17th century that gave rise to Dublin's literary reputation. Restoration dramatists such as George Farquhar were followed 50 years later by the brilliant satirist Jonathan Swift. The late 19th century saw the emergence of Oscar Wilde, whose epigrams enthralled the world. William Butler Yeats, encouraged by the flourishing Irish literary movement, helped found the Abbey Theatre, which opened in 1904. George Bernard Shaw, and subsequent writers such as James Joyce, Samuel Beckett and Brendan Behan continued the literary tradition.

Displays Photographs, paintings and other items associated with Ireland's literary titans are backed up with explanatory material. First editions and rare volumes abound, and treasures include original letters of the poet Thomas Moore, a manuscript of W.B. Yeats and an indenture signed by Jonathan Swift. The collection is housed in a spectacular 18th-century mansion, and has an excellent bookshop, Volumes.

THE BASICS

writersmuseum.com

✚ G5

✉ 18 Parnell Square North

☎ 872 2077

🕐 Mon–Sat 10–5, Sun and public hols 11–5

🚉 Connolly

🚍 Cross-city buses

♿ Ground floor good (a few steps into the building)

✋ Moderate

❓ Excellent audio guide

HIGHLIGHTS

● Letters of Thomas Moore and Maria Edgeworth
● Yeats manuscript
● Indenture signed by Swift
● Painted ceiling and doors in the Gallery of Writers
● Bookshop with Irish works

EPIC Ireland

- Ship voyage sculpture
- Irish music footage
- Sporting heroes exhibits
- Famous faces

An audiovisual feast that tells the story of the Irish diaspora, this 21st-century visitor experience in a former 19th-century wine and tobacco warehouse presents a series of spaces and displays in brick-lined vaults.

Sculptures and displays Themed around the astounding fact that the Irish diaspora is one of the world's largest, the 20 immersive galleries tell the stories of the many millions of people who left Ireland due to events such as the Irish famine in the mid-19th century. A huge, striking sculpture depicts the history of their epic sea journeys. Elsewhere in the subterranean galleries, a series of interactive exhibitions, with touch screens, sound and installations, have four themes: Migration,

EPIC Ireland is a 21st-century sensory spectacle occupying a vast warehouse space that was built in the 19th century by pioneering Scottish engineer John Rennie

Motivation, Influence and Connection. One section looks at famous people of Irish descent such as JFK, Billy the Kid, Grace Kelly and Charles de Gaulle. There is also a section devoted to Irish music and dance and how its influences have spread around the world. It's not all about heroes; the Rogue's Gallery highlights the bad boys, with an Irish outlaws quiz. The CHQ Building (▷ 59) has its own history and was the location for the 1856 Crimean War Banquet.

Genealogy section Part of EPIC Ireland is the Irish Family History Centre, where visitors can search for their Irish ancestors using the latest digital technology. Visitors can have a 15-minute consultation with a genealogy expert and use the interactive displays to research their heritage.

THE BASICS

epicchq.com

🚩 J6

✉ CHQ Building, Custom House Quay

☎ 531 3688

🕐 Daily 10–6.45 (last entry 5)

🚉 Connolly

🚌 Cross-city buses; Luas George's Dock

♿ Excellent

💷 Expensive

❓ Gift shop

GPO Witness History

GPO Witness History brings alive the dramatic events that took place in 1916

THE BASICS

gpowitnesshistory.ie

H6

GPO, O'Connell Street

872 1916

Mon–Fri 10–5.30,
Sun 12–5.30. Last
admission 4.30

Café

Cross-city buses; Luas
Abbey Street

Good

Expensive

HIGHLIGHTS

● *Fire and Steel* movie
● Bullet holes in pillars
● Copy of the 1916
Proclamation of the Irish
Republic

The scene of momentous events in Ireland's political history, the General Post Office building, in a prominent spot on broad O'Connell Street, symbolizes the birthplace of modern Ireland.

Scene of siege The historic building was designed by Irish architect Francis Johnston, with statues by John Smith that dominate the skyline. Inside, the reading of the Proclamation of the Irish Republic took place during the Easter Rising of 1916. The insurgents were forced to surrender after the interior was reduced to rubble—bullet holes on the portico columns are a reminder of the bitter struggle—and 16 insurgents were later executed.

Exhibition The main building is still a working post office, but its north side now houses the GPO Witness History exhibition, a permanent visitor attraction. With immersive exhibits, documents, photos and film footage, this re-creates the events that took place here during the momentous Easter Week. Don't miss the excellent short film, *Fire and Steel*, which uses original photographs and re-created scenes of events that took place in and around the GPO on that fateful day. It reflects events on both sides of the conflict, through the eyes of bystanders caught in the crossfire. On the wall is a rare copy of the 1916 proclamation. The new Thomas F. Meagher Exhibition, upstairs, describes the creation of Ireland's tricolor national flag, and its symbolism of peace.

James Joyce Centre

You will find all things Joycean at the James Joyce Centre

Of all those to grace the Dublin scene during the 20th century, James Joyce has undoubtedly earned the greatest reputation internationally, so it is fitting that a whole house is devoted to the writer.

Connections This beautifully restored 18th-century house, in an impressive street of Georgian redbrick residences off O'Connell Street, is home to this cultural center. Initially, its Joycean connection was established through a dancing master called Denis J. Maginni, who leased one of the rooms in the house around the turn of the 20th century and appears as a character in *Ulysses*. Tours of the house are available and include the opportunity to listen to tapes of "Uncle James," reading from *Ulysses* and *Finnegans Wake*.

Memorabilia Start your visit on the top floor where there's an atmospheric display of re-created period rooms, videos and computer installations, as well as items relating to Joyce's life and work, including furniture from the Paris apartment where he lived when he worked on his masterpiece, *Finnegans Wake*. The front door out in the courtyard was rescued from the now demolished No. 7 Eccles Street, Leopold and Molly Bloom's address in *Ulysses*. Check for Joycean-themed 90-minute walking tours of Dublin departing from the venue. The center is also home to a permanent exhibition "James Joyce & *Ulysses*," an interactive exhibition that was previously at the National Library.

THE BASICS

jamesjoyce.ie
⊞ H5
✉ 35 North Great George's Street
☎ 878 8547
🕐 Mon–Sat 10–5, Sun 12–5; closed Mon Oct–Mar
🍴 Café
🚆 Connolly
🚌 Cross-city buses
🚻 Few
✋ Moderate
❓ Guided tours of house and Joycean Dublin

HIGHLIGHTS

● Joyce family members
● Recordings
● Library
● James Joyce & *Ulysses* exhibition
● No. 7 Eccles Street door
● Copy of Joyce's death mask

Jameson Distillery Bow St.

Barrels bear the name of this famous distillery; the distillery's main entrance

THE BASICS

jamesonwhiskey.com

⊞ F6

✉ Bow Street, Smithfield

☎ 807 2355

🕑 May–Oct Mon–Thu and Sun 10–6, Fri–Sat 10–7; Nov–Apr Mon–Thu and Sun 10–5.30, Fri–Sat 10–6.30 (last tour)

🍴 Restaurant, café and bar

🚌 Cross-city buses; Luas Smithfield

♿ Good

✋ Expensive

ℹ Gift shop

HIGHLIGHTS

● Whiskey tasting from the barrel
● Immersive guided tours
● Historic 18th-century building
● JJs Bar

Reopened in March 2017 after major restoration, this historical landmark was formerly known as Old Jameson Distillery. As its old name suggests, it sits in the original whiskey distillery buildings, dating back to 1780.

History With brick walls, the original stills and immense vats, the distillery presents a step back in time through one of Ireland's most popular products. Jameson was the country's most famous distillery, in operation from 1780 to 1971, until it transferred to the Midleton Distillery in Cork. John Jameson, who was from Scotland, and his son (also John) became manager of the family brewery belonging to his wife, Mary Stein. The original equipment showcases the method used to produce whiskey.

Tours and tastings Jameson's new-look attraction features cutting-edge technology—in complete contrast to the historic surroundings. It has a choice of fully immersive guided tours: The Bow St. Experience focuses on Jameson's rich heritage with comparative whiskey tasting; the 90-minute Whiskey Blending Class lets you taste premium whiskeys blended by masters, and you can also blend your own to take home. A highlight is the cask draw and tasting in the maturation warehouse. There is also a Whiskey Cocktail Making Class. Guides will explain how Irish whiskey is unique in its triple distillation. The main entrance is dominated by JJ's Bar, where all tours end with a complimentary drink.

National Museum — Decorative Arts & History

Here you can view the decorative arts and social history collections of the National Museum—products of Irish artists and craftspeople that were hidden from view for many years.

The building Sir Thomas Burgh (1670–1730), the architect of the Old Library in Trinity College (▷ 72–73), also designed Dublin's large Royal Barracks, just over 1.5km (a mile) outside the city. Built in 1704, on high ground overlooking the River Liffey, they were handed over in 1922 to the Irish State, which named them after Michael Collins, the revolutionary leader killed in an ambush toward the end of the Civil War. Until decommissioning in 1988, they were generally thought to be the oldest military barracks still in use anywhere in the world.

Exhibits The barracks opened as an annex to the National Museum in 1997, strengthening Dublin's cultural and historical focus. The items on display range from the 17th century up to the present day and comprise Irish silver, glass and furniture, all of which reached a high point of artistic excellence in the 18th century. Don't miss the Chinese porcelain Fonthill vase, which has managed to survive its well-documented wanderings in Asia and Europe, or the Persian and Venetian art nouveau items in the "What's In Store" collection. Permanent exhibitions include "The Way We Wore," 250 years of Irish clothing and jewelry, and a homage to the influential designer and architect Eileen Gray.

THE BASICS

museum.ie
🔲 E6
✉ Benburb Street
☎ 677 7444
🕐 Tue–Sat 10–5, Sun 2–5
🍴 Café
🚆 Heuston
🚌 25, 25A, 66, 67, 90; Luas Museum
♿ Very good
🎫 Free
❓ Book tours in advance (inexpensive)

HIGHLIGHTS

● Old barracks building
● Fonthill vase
● What's in Store
● "The Way We Wore" exhibition
● Curator's Choice

THE NORTH TOP 25

55

More to See

14 HENRIETTA STREET

14henriettastreet.ie

Step back into three centuries of Dublin's social history at this well-preserved, atmospheric house, from its grand Georgian beginnings to its use as a cramped 20th-century tenement building. Guided tours take you through personal stories of its former residents, using audio, film and archives.

➕ F5 ⊠ 14 Henrietta Street ☎ 524 0383 🕒 Wed–Sun 10–4 (hourly tours) 🚌 Bus 83, 83a; Luas Dominick 💷 Expensive

CUSTOM HOUSE

Designed by James Gandon in 1791, the Custom House is an outstanding example of Georgian architecture and one of Dublin's finest buildings. Burned down by the IRA in 1921, it has now been beautifully restored.

➕ J6 ⊠ Custom House Quay ☎ 888 2538 🕒 Not open to the public at time of publishing 🚉 Tara Street 🚌 Cross-city buses; Luas Busáras 🔵 Good 💷 Inexpensive

DOCKLANDS

docklands.ie

The redevelopment of the former docks stretches east along the north side of the Liffey from the Custom House to North Wall Quay, with developments on the south bank, too, linked by the Sean O' Casey Bridge (2005) and the Samuel Beckett Bridge (2009). Living, working and retail spaces are popping up, fueled by an influx of new IT and finance businesses.

➕ J6–M6 ⊠ North of the Liffey 🚉 Tara Street 🚌 Cross-city buses; Luas Connolly Station

FAMINE MEMORIAL

A series of emaciated figures along the quays commemorates the Great Famine of 1845–49, a devastating period in Irish history when around 1 million people died. The sculptures were created by Dublin artist Rowan Gillespie. Look for the World Poverty Stone.

➕ J6 ⊠ Custom House Quay 🚉 Tara Street 🚌 Cross-city buses; Luas Busáras

The statue Children of Lír

A 1900s display at 14 Henrietta Street

THE NORTH   MORE TO SEE

FOUR COURTS

Home to the Irish law courts since 1796, the Four Courts has much in common with the Custom House—primarily its designer, James Gandon. This Dublin landmark also suffered fire damage during the turbulent events of 1921. Visits are permitted only when courts are in session.

🕂 F6 ✉ Inns Quay ☎ 888 6000
🚌 Cross-city buses; Luas Four Courts
♿ Few 🎟 Free

GARDEN OF REMEMBRANCE

The statue of the *Children of Lír* is the focal point of this contemplative garden, dedicated to those who died in pursuit of Irish independence. A poignant Irish fairy tale, about three children turned into swans by a wicked stepmother, inspired Oisín Kelly's bronze sculpture (1971).

🕂 G5 ✉ Garden of Remembrance, Parnell Square East ☎ 821 3021 🚌 Cross-city buses

JEANIE JOHNSTON

jeaniejohnston.ie
This is an authentic replica of the *Jeanie Johnston*, a tall ship that made 16 journeys from Ireland to North America between 1847 and 1855, carrying approximately 2,500 poverty-stricken Irish emigrants fleeing the potato famine. Visitors can see re-created scenes from those challenging journeys in the cramped sleeping quarters and on the once-crowded deck.

🕂 J/K6 ✉ Custom House Quay, North Dock ☎ 473 0111 🕐 Daily 10–5 🚇 Tara Street 🚌 Cross-city buses; Luas George's Dock 🎟 Expensive

ST. MARY'S PRO CATHEDRAL

procathedral.ie
Mother church for Catholic Dublin, affectionately known as "the Pro," this impressive 1825 building has hosted many Church and State occasions. Sunday mass is sung by the Palestrina Choir.

🕂 H5 ✉ Marlborough Street ☎ 874 5441 🕐 Mon–Fri 9.30–5, Sat 9.30 to after eve Mass, Sun 9–1 and 5 to after eve Mass 🚌 Cross-city buses; Luas Abbey Street

ST. MICHAN'S CHURCH

A functioning parish church, St. Michan's is best known for its burial vaults. Here lie the mummified remains of some of Dublin's famous—and infamous—characters from the 17th to 19th centuries, including earls and a Crusader. Bram Stoker, author of *Dracula*, was said to have come here with his family. There are regular tours of the vaults and the church, which contains a pipe organ.

🕂 F6 ✉ Church Road ☎ 872 4154 🕐 Mid-Mar to Oct Mon–Fri 10–12.45, 2–4.30; Nov to mid-Mar 12.30–3.30; Sat 10–12.45 year round 🚌 Cross-city buses; Luas Four Courts

THE SPIRE

Also known as the Monument of Light, this striking spire was unveiled in 2003 and is a prominent landmark. Standing at 120m (394ft) high, and made of reflective stainless steel which changes hue throughout the day and night, it stands on the site of Nelson's Column, opposite the General Post Office (▷ 52).

🕂 H6 ✉ O'Connell Street 🚌 Cross-city buses; Luas Abbey Street

A Walk North of the River

This walk is in the northern district of Dublin, which is undergoing a major rejuvenation. It also takes in part of the quays.

DISTANCE: 2km (1.25 miles) **ALLOW:** 1 hour plus stops

START

GRESHAM HOTEL (▷ 112)
 H5 🚌 Cross-city buses

① Start at the Gresham Hotel (▷ 112) on O'Connell Street. Facing the hotel, turn right and walk south on O'Connell Street toward the quayside.

② Continue to the General Post Office (▷ 52) and look up for the Spire (▷ 57), a metallic monument that changes color slightly throughout the day and night.

③ Opposite the Spire go left into Henry Street, passing Moore Street and its market barrows. Halfway down Henry Street is the Ilac shopping mall (▷ 59). Turn onto Mary Street.

④ Continue along Mary Street and at the T-junction at the end turn left into Capel Street. Walk on over two roads down to the quayside.

END

JAMESON DISTILLERY BOW ST.
(▷ 54)  F6 🚌 68, 69, 79, 90; Luas Smithfield

⑧ At the end, turn right into Bow Street where you will find Jameson Distillery Bow St. (▷ 54). Outside, climb the 244 winding steps to the top of the Viewing Tower (obtain tickets via the Generator Hostel) for great views.

⑦ Take the next right, Church Street. Cross the road and you will see St. Michan's Church (▷ 57) on your left, famous for the mummified bodies in its crypt. Continue to the traffic lights and turn left into May Lane.

⑥ To your right is the fine Georgian building of the Four Courts (▷ 57).

⑤ In front of you is the Grattan Bridge, lined with sculpted sea horses. Turn right along the quay, passing the next bridge, O'Donovan Rossa Bridge, and into Inns Quay.

Shopping

ARRAN STREET EAST

arranstreeteast.ie

Hand-thrown pottery is the main feature here, with mugs, jugs and pots in simple, striking designs. The studio also has a lovely café.

➕ G6 ✉ 1 Little Green Street ☎ 083 814 6672 🚌 Cross-city buses; Luas Four Courts

CHAPTERS BOOKSHOP

chapters.ie

Ireland's largest independent bookstore, has a vast array of new and second-hand titles including literature and politics, plus CDs and DVDs.

➕ G5 ✉ Ivy Exchange, Parnell Street ☎ 879 2700 🚌 Cross-city buses; Luas Parnell

THE CHQ BUILDING

chq.ie

A 19th-century wine and tobacco store is now a mall of smart boutiques, shops, coffee bars and Mitchell & Sons, Dublin's oldest fine wine merchants.

➕ J6 ✉ IFSC, George's Dock ☎ 673 6054 🚊 Tara Street 🚌 Cross-city buses; Luas Busáras

EASON

eason.ie

This vast bookstore, the largest in the Eason chain, has a huge selection of books and magazines as well as with stationery, art equipment and music. There is also a café.

➕ H6 ✉ 40 Lower O'Connell Street ☎ 858 3800 🚊 Tara Street or Connolly 🚌 Cross-city buses

ILAC CENTRE

ilac.ie

Dublin's longest-established shopping mall is a labyrinth of small shops and high street names such as Dunnes.

➕ G6 ✉ Henry Street ☎ 828 8900 🚊 Tara Street 🚌 Cross-city buses; Luas Jervis

JENNIFER SLATTERY TEXTILE

jenniferslattery.com

This studio specializes in timeless pieces—shirts and scarves to embroidered table runners—created from Irish linen and wool by local weavers. It occupies an attractive Victorian building in Smithfield.

➕ E6 ✉ 74 Benburb Street ☎ 086 075 4086 🚌 Cross-city buses; Luas Museum

LOUIS COPELAND

louiscopeland.com

This is the flagship store of the renowned gentlemen's outfitter selling suits coats, shirts and ties. A Louis Copeland suit, made to measure or off the peg, is a rite of passage for the well-dressed Irishman.

➕ G6 ✉ 39–41 Capel Street ☎ 872 1600 🚊 Tara Street 🚌 Cross-city buses

WINDING STAIR

winding-stair.com

A literary landmark overlooking Ha'penny Bridge, this quaint independent bookstore offers a wide range of new and second-hand books. There is also a delightful restaurant upstairs (▷ 62).

➕ G6 ✉ 40 Lower Ormond Quay ☎ 872 6576 🚊 Tara Street 🚌 Cross-city buses

CRAFTSMANSHIP

Dublin's rich reputation as a hub of creative excellence dates back several centuries. Irish furniture and silver of the Georgian period embody some of the finest craftsmanship of the late 18th and early 19th centuries (the harp in the hallmark indicates a piece was made in Ireland), and early 20th-century Irish art has attracted worldwide acclaim. Antiques fairs take place regularly.

Entertainment and Nightlife

3ARENA

3arena.ie

This state-of-the-art entertainment venue in Docklands attracts top names in music and comedy. It also stages musicals, opera and concerts.

🚇 M6 ✉ North Wall Quay ☎ 819 8888 🚌 151; Luas Docklands Station

ABBEY THEATRE

abbeytheatre.ie

Founded in 1904, the national theater played a vital role in the renaissance of Irish culture. Today, the quality of the performances and playwriting of Irish works is world-class.

🚇 H6 ✉ 26 Abbey Street Lower ☎ 878 7222 🚆 Connolly/Tara Street 🚌 Cross-city buses

BAR 1661

bar1661.ie

This new cocktail bar pays homage to *poitín* (potcheen)—1661 was the year the native spirit was banned in Ireland. Try its sophisticated concoctions such as Angels Boutique: *poitín*, toasted barley, apple and sherry.

🚇 G6 ✉ 1–5 Green Street ☎ 878 8706 🚌 Cross-city buses

THE COBBLESTONE

cobblestonepub.ie

A traditional pub with regular music sessions, including Irish, blues and folk, this bar has been a Smithfield fixture for many years. There are nightly sessions, plus afternoon music at weekends.

🚇 E6 ✉ 77 King Street North ☎ 872 1799 🚌 Cross-city buses; Luas Smithfield

GATE THEATRE

gate-theatre.ie

Some of Dublin's most inspired and sophisticated plays are performed in this 18th-century building. The theater's actors, playwrights and productions tour the world.

🚇 G5 ✉ Cavendish Row, Parnell Square ☎ 874 4045 🚆 Connolly 🚌 Cross-city buses

LAUGHTER LOUNGE

laughterlounge.com

Treat yourself to a good giggle with a host of both local and international stand-up talent on Thursday, Friday and Saturday nights.

🚇 H6 ✉ 4–8 Eden Quay ☎ 878 3003 🚆 Tara Street 🚌 Cross-city buses

LIGHTHOUSE CINEMA

lighthousecinema.ie

This independent cinema has most of the latest major releases, plus short films and a program of live screenings of opera, ballet and theater.

🚇 E6 ✉ Market Square, Smithfield ☎ 872 8006 🚌 Cross-city buses; Luas Smithfields

PANTI BAR

pantibar.com

One of the first LGBTQ+ bars in Dublin, Panti Bar's neon and scarlet interior hosts cheeky entertainment across its two floors. There is live entertainment most nights, ranging from DJs to cabaret acts and drag shows.

🚇 G6 ✉ 7–8 Capel Street ☎ 874 0710 🚌 Cross-city buses; Luas Jervis

THE VIRGIN MARY

louisfitzgerald.com

Ireland's first alcohol-free bar, this stylish venue serves booze-free cocktails, wines, and a Raven Nitro Coffee, which mimics the texture and appearance of Guinness. Despite it being alcohol-free, entrance here is for over-18s only.

🚇 G6 ✉ 54 Capel Street ☎ 086 245 8392 🚌 Cross-city buses; Luas Jervis

Where to Eat

PRICES

Prices are approximate, based on a 3-course meal for one person.

€€€ over €50
€€ €30–€50
€ under €30

BESHOFF'S (€)

beshoffrestaurant.com

Great fish and hand-cut chips (including gluten-free) with catch-of-the-day fresh specials at this Dublin institution. Grab a window seat for views of the Spire and GPO.

✚ H6 ✉ 6 Upper O'Connell Street
☎ 872 4400 ◉ Breakfast, lunch and dinner daily 🚉 Connolly 🚌 Cross-city buses; Luas Abbey Street

LE BON CRUBEEN (€€)

leboncrubeen.ie

The brasserie menu at Le Bon Crubeen is always top class. Best ingredients from Irish suppliers, including steaks and oysters, are used in European-influenced dishes. The pre-theater menu here is handy for those heading to the Gate or 3Arena.

✚ H5 ✉ 81–82 Talbot Street ☎ 704 0126
◉ Lunch and dinner daily 🚉 Connolly
🚌 Cross-city buses; Luas Connolly

BROTHER HUBBARD (€–€€)

brotherhubbard.ie

European and Turkish-influenced dishes feature and there's a deliciously different brunch menu. It's furnished with exposed brick, wooden tables, stools and banquettes.

✚ G6 ✉ 153 Capel Street ☎ 441 1112
◉ Breakfast and lunch Mon–Fri and Sun, breakfast, lunch and dinner Tue–Sat 🚉 Connolly 🚌 Cross-city buses; Luas Abbey Street

CHAPTER ONE (€€€)

chapteronerestaurant.com

One of Dublin's most elegant restaurants occupies the basement of the Dublin Writers Museum. It's a real treat. Irish contemporary food meets French classic cooking, using top quality local produce. There is a good selection of wines from around the world.

✚ G5 ✉ 18–19 Parnell Square ☎ 873 2266
◉ Lunch Tue–Fri, dinner Tue–Sat 🚉 Connolly
🚌 Cross-city buses

ELY BAR & GRILL (€€)

elywinebar.ie

Located inside stone-walled wine vaults, Ely's offers a huge selection of wines by the glass, along with an extensive menu of contemporary Irish meat and fish dishes. There is also a waterside terrace to enjoy.

✚ J6 ✉ CHQ Building, IFSC ☎ 672 0010
◉ Daily noon–late 🚌 Cross-city buses; Luas Connolly

FISH SHOP (€€)

fish-shop.ie

Pull up a stool at the counter of this little restaurant, serving seafood classics such as beer-battered fish and chips, and local mussels and cockles, plus excellent bar snacks and wines by the glass.

✚ E6 ✉ 76 Benburb Street ☎ 557 1473
◉ Lunch Tue–Sun, daily dinner 🚌 Cross-city buses; Luas Smithfield

L. MULLIGAN GROCER (€€)

lmulligangrocer1.weebly.com

Dark and cozy, this gastropub in trendy Stoneybatter has an excellent menu, with Scotch eggs (veggie version too), and mackerel with capers. There's no Guinness here—try its Irish craft beer tasting flight.

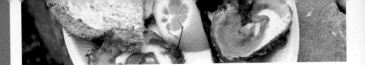

✉ 18 Stoneybatter ☎ 670 9889
🕐 Lunch Sat and Sun, daily dinner 🚌 37, 39, 39a, 70

MR FOX (€€)

www.mrfox.ie

A stylishly informal bar and dining room. Expect imaginative seasonal dishes, such as crab, kohlrabi and smoked eel starter, and mains of venison, smoked pear and black pudding.

✚ G4 ✉ 38 Parnell Square W ☎ 874 7778
🕐 Wed–Sat lunch and dinner; Tue dinner only

MV CILL AIRNE (€€)

mvcillairne.com

This historic little ship moored in Docklands, in Quay 16, has a good restaurant serving European dishes, plus a bistro and bar. Convenient for the 3Arena.

✚ K6 ✉ Quay 16, North Wall Quay ☎ 817 8760 🕐 Daily lunch and dinner 🚆 Docklands Station 🚊 Luas Busáras

ONE SOCIETY (€)

onesociety.ie

In the evenings this friendly place with huge picture windows morphs from a coffee and brunch spot (daily until 3pm) to a lively restaurant serving great pizzas, including popular vegan options.

✚ H5 ✉ 1 Lower Gardiner Street ☎ 537 5261 🕐 Tue–Sun breakfast, lunch and dinner 🚌 Cross-city buses; Luas Parnell

TERRA MADRE (€€)

terramadre.ie

Come to this informal café-restaurant for authentic, rustic Italian cuisine, using high-quality ingredients including its olive oils and hand-made egg pastas.

✚ G6 ✉ 13a Bachelors Walk ☎ 873 5300
🕐 Daily lunch and dinner 🚌 Cross-city buses; Luas GPO/O'Connell

VEGINITY (€–€€)

veginity.com

Dublin has come a long way in recent years to add to the trend of good plant-based eating places. Tasty vegan dishes are on offer at this bright new café, including an all-day breakfast, pastries made by their own pastry chef and organic wines.

✚ G4 ✉ 101 Upper Dorset Street ☎ 535 9067 🕐 Wed–Sun breakfast, lunch and dinner 🚌 Cross-city buses

THE WINDING STAIR (€€)

winding-stair.com

Overlooking the river, and above the bookshop of the same name (▷ 59), this quaint restaurant serves tasty dishes such as smoked ox tongue and black pudding hash cake.

✚ G6 ✉ 40 Ormond Quay Lower ☎ 872 7320 🕐 Daily lunch and dinner 🚊 Tara Street 🚌 Cross-city buses; Luas Jervis

THE WOOLLEN MILLS (€€)

thewoollenmills.com

Overlooking the Liffey, this restaurant is spread over four floors, including a roof terrace. In addition to its all-day menu of Irish dishes with vegan options, there's a bakery on site.

✚ G6 ✉ 42 Ormond Quay Lower ☎ 828 0835 🕐 Mon–Sat breakfast, daily lunch and dinner 🚌 Cross-city buses; Luas Jervis

YAMAMORI (€€)

yamamori.ie

One of three branches of a Japanese chain, this Northside outlet specializes in sushi and *nigiri*, plus grill items and ramen and occasional late-night events.

✚ G6 ✉ 38–39 Ormond Quay Upper ☎ 872 0003 🕐 Mon–Fri dinner; Sat and Sun lunch and dinner 🚌 Cross-city buses; Luas Jervis

The Southeast

This district, south of the River Liffey, has been Dublin's most elegant and fashionable area since the 18th century. Here you will find Trinity College, the national museums and elegant Georgian squares.

Top 25

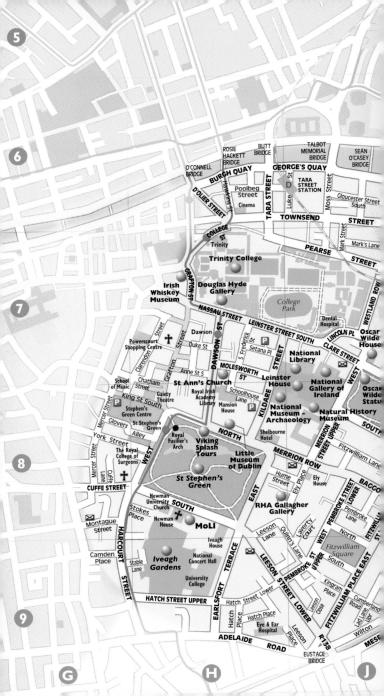

5

6

7

8

9

ROSIE
HACKETT
BRIDGE

BUTT
BRIDGE

TALBOT
MEMORIAL
BRIDGE

SEÁN
O'CASEY
BRIDGE

O'CONNELL
BRIDGE

BURGH QUAY

GEORGE'S QUAY

D'OLIER STREET

Poolbeg
Street

Cinema

TARA STREET

George's St

TARA
STREET
STATION

Luke St

Moss Street

Gloucester Street
South

TOWNSEND

STREET

Mark Street

Mark's Lane

COLLEGE ST

Trinity

PEARSE

STREET

GRAFTON ST

Trinity College

Irish
Whiskey
Museum

Douglas Hyde
Gallery

College Park

Dental
Hospital

WESTLAND ROW

NASSAU STREET

LEINSTER STREET SOUTH

LINCOLN PL

Oscar
Wilde
House

Dawson

Clarendon Street

Grafton Street

Dawson Street

Duke St

Powerscourt
Shopping Centre

School
of Music

Chatham
Street

Anne St S

MOLESWORTH

St Frederick
St

Setana Pl

National
Library

CLARE STREET

KILDARE STREET

National
Gallery of
Ireland

Oscar
Wilde
Statue

St Ann's Church

Gaiety
Theatre

Royal Irish
Academy
Library

Schoolhouse
Lane

Leinster
House

National
Museum -
Archaeology

Natural
History
Museum

MERRION STREET UPPER

SOUTH

Mercer Street

King St South

P

Stephen's
Green Centre

St Stephen's
Green

Mansion
House

P

Shelbourne
Hotel

Fitzwilliam Lane

York Street

Glovers
Alley

St Stephen's
Green

Royal
Fusilier's
Arch

Viking
Splash
Tours

NORTH

Little
Museum
of Dublin

MERRION ROW

The Royal
College of Surgeons

WEST

EAST

Hume
Street

Ely Place

Ely
House

PEMBROKE STREET LOWER

BAGGO

CUFFE STREET

Cuffe
Lane

St Stephen's
Green

RHA Gallagher
Gallery

Laverty
Court

WEST

North

FITZW

Montague
Street

Newman
University
Church

SOUTH

Newman
House

MoLI

Stokes
Place

Leeson
Lane

Quinn's Lane

Fitzwilliam
Square
South

Pembroke
Lane

Camden
Place

Stable
Lane

Iveagh
Gardens

Iveagh
House

National
Concert Hall

University
College

EARLSFORT TERRACE

LEESON STREET LOWER

PEMBROKE ST UPPER

Leeson
Close

Kingram
Place

Cumberland
Road

FITZWILLIAM PLACE EAST

R138

HARCOURT STREET

HATCH STREET UPPER

Hatch
Place

Hatch Street Lower

Hatch Place

Eye & Ear
Hospital

Leeson
Place

Wilton

MES

ADELAIDE

ROAD

EUSTACE
BRIDGE

G

H

J

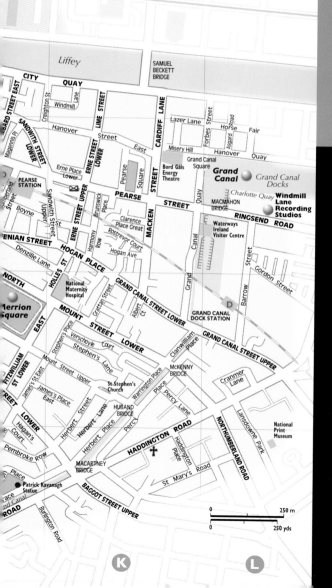

Liffey

CITY QUAY

SAMUEL BECKETT BRIDGE

SANDWITH STREET LOWER

Magennis Pl

Creighton St

Windmill Lane

Hanover Street

LIME STREET

ERNE STREET LOWER

CARDIFF LANE

Lazer Lane

Forbes Street

Horse Road

Asgard Road

Fair Street

Misery Hill

Hanover Quay

East

PEARSE STATION

Cumberland Street

Boyne

Sandwith St Upper

Erne Place Lower

ERNE STREET UPPER

Brunswick Place

Pearse Square

Bord Gáis Energy Theatre

Grand Canal Square

Grand Canal

Grand Canal Docks

PEARSE STREET

MACKEN STREET

Charlotte Quay

MACMAHON BRIDGE

RINGSEND ROAD

Windmill Lane Recording Studios

FENIAN STREET

Denzille Lane

HOGAN PLACE

Clarence Place Great

Harmony Row

Rostrevor Court

Hogan Ave

Waterways Ireland Visitor Centre

Grand Canal Quay

Grand Canal

Street

Gordon Street

NORTH

Merrion Square

EAST

HOLLES ST

National Maternity Hospital

Grattan Street

MOUNT STREET LOWER

GRAND CANAL STREET LOWER

Albert Ct

GRAND CANAL DOCK STATION

Barrow Street

GRAND CANAL STREET UPPER

D

FITZWILLIAM ST LOWER

STREET LOWER

Stephen's Place

Verschoyle Court

Mount Street Upper

James's St East

James's Place East

Stephen's Lane

St Stephen's Church

Warrington Place

Clanwilliam Place

Percy Place

McKENNY BRIDGE

Cranmer Lane

Hagan's Court

Pembroke Row

Herbert Street

Herbert Lane

HUBAND BRIDGE

Herbert Place

Percy Lane

Percy

HADDINGTON ROAD

Haddington Place

NORTHUMBERLAND ROAD

Lansdowne Park

National Print Museum

Place

Patrick Kavanagh Statue

ROAD

Burlington Road

MACARTNEY BRIDGE

St Mary's Road

BAGGOT STREET UPPER

0   250 m

0   250 yds

K

L

The Little Museum of Dublin

TOP 25

Discover all things good or bad about 20th-century Dublin at this pint-size museum

THE BASICS

littlemuseum.ie

✚ H8

✉ 15 St. Stephen's Green

🕐 Daily 9.30–5, Thu 9.30–8

☎ 661 1000

🚌 Cross-city buses; Luas St. Stephen's Green

♿ Good

🍽 Moderate

❓ Guided tours only, hourly

HIGHLIGHTS

● 1916 Uprising photos
● Letter written by James Joyce in 1902
● Soccer photos
● Georgian House Party, every Fri 6–7pm

This gem of a museum is a collection of myriad items telling the story of the Irish capital through its people. Its launch was preceded with an appeal to the public to donate 20th-century historical objects relating to the city, and the response was overwhelming.

Photos and documents Excellent guided tours take you through the history of Dublin over the 20th century, from photographs of Queen Victoria's visit in 1900, to the global pop sensation of U2. There are more than 5,000 artifacts donated by Dubliners since 2011. You'll also find exhibits about the 1907 International Exhibition in Herbert Park, and evidence of the desperate poverty of some of Dublin's tenement housing. Fascinating material tells the story of the potato famine and the 1916 Uprising, including a souvenir propoganda placard. Other items on show include a slightly morbid display of writer James Joyces's death mask from 1941.

Sports stars Photos also tell the story of Ireland's sporting achievements, including a photo of the Ireland soccer team before they played against Hungary—and posing the question of were they giving a fascist salute?—and Ireland's most successful soccer team, Shamrock Rovers FC, complete with their striped shirts and socks from 1954. There are some excellent temporary exhibitions, too, plus walking tours of nearby St. Stephen's Green.

about Ireland's
ry heritage at
n's new 21st-
ry museum

TOP
25

MoLI – Museum of Literature Ireland

This new museum, a decade in the making, pays homage to Ireland's literary greatness. Its three floors display a series of exhibitions incorporating words, film and sound to celebrate the works of the country's famous writers.

Venue UCD Newman House, on St. Stephen's Green, was the home of the Catholic University of Ireland, which then became University College Dublin (UCD). The museum incorporates two graceful Georgian townhouses, with exquisite baroque plasterwork by the Lafranchini brothers and rococo stuccowork.

Displays The immersive displays explore Ireland's deep literary heritage, from early storytelling to great contemporary writers. The Riverrun of Language installation is an all-surrounding wall of sound of—recorded readings of Irish writing, from folklore to the present day. There are some priceless literary pieces—notably, the very first copy of James Joyce's *Ulysses*, in a glass case on the top floor. A handwritten letter from James Joyce to W.B. Yeats, asking for help to publish *Dubliners*, is framed on the wall. Dublin city is also honored.

Outside The light and airy rooms have huge windows that look out onto the museum's hidden gardens, where a café backs onto the tranquil Iveagh Gardens (▷ 74). Note that MoLI is pronounced "Molly"—a nod to Molly Bloom, heroine of Joyce's *Ulysses*.

THE BASICS

moli.ie

✚ H8

✉ 86 St. Stephen's Green

☎ 477 9811

🕐 Daily 10–6

🍴 Café

🚇 Pearse

🚌 Cross-city buses; Luas St. Stephen's Green

♿ Good

✋ Moderate

HIGHLIGHTS

● The first copy of James Joyces' *Ulysses*
● Museum gardens
● Ornate, Italian stucco plasterwork
● The Commons Café

National Gallery of Ireland

The National Gallery's imposing entrance (left); Grand Gallery, Dargan Wing (right)

THE BASICS

nationalgallery.ie
➕ J7
✉ Merrion Square West
☎ 661 5133
🕐 Mon and Sun 11–5.30, Tue–Sat 9.15–5.30, Thu 9.15–8.30
🍴 Café
🚊 Pearse
🚌 Cross-city buses; Luas St. Stephen's Green
♿ Very good
💷 Free, special exhibitions expensive
❓ Public tours Thu 6.30pm, Sat 12.30 and 2.30, Sun 11.30, 12.30, 1.30

HIGHLIGHTS

● The Shaw Room
● Covered courtyard
● National Portrait Collection
● Monet, *Argenteuil Basin*
● Jack B. Yeats, *The Liffey Swim*
● Caravaggio, *The Taking of Christ*

The gallery is the home of one of Europe's premier collections of Old Masters—even better after a multimillion euro refurbishment, taking six years and completed in 2017.

Origins Facing Merrion Square and the lawns of Leinster House, the gallery opened in 1864 to display old master paintings to inspire Irish artists of the period. Its content has expanded—there are now more than 16,300 works of art, including the nation's collection of Irish and European fine art from the early Renaissance to the present day.

Refurbishment The major alterations show off the building in all its glory, its architects Heneghan Peng having expertly combined its original 19th-century features with a contemporary edge. There is now more exhibiting space, better use of natural light, and stunning new areas such as the once-hidden courtyard that connects the Dargan and 1901 Milltown wings. The Shaw Room has been transformed, flooded with natural light from the reestablished four huge windows, which hark back to the days when the room was a sculpture gallery.

Artworks Level 1 is devoted to the Irish collection, displayed chronologically from the 17th to the 20th centuries, with a focus on Jack B. Yeats and John Lavery. One room features Irish stained glass, including the renowned Harry Clarke. Level 3 has a large European collection.

National Museum — Archaeology

_The Museum's gal-
leried exhibition room
(left); majestic external
stonework (right)_

This branch of the National Museum houses most of Ireland's greatest archeological treasures. A visit here is a must for a deeper understanding of the country's prehistoric history and culture.

Extensive collections For more than a century, the National Museum (1890) has faced the National Library across the square leading to the Dáil, or Houses of Parliament. The museum contains Western Europe's most extensive collection of prehistoric gold ornaments, mostly dating from the Bronze Age (c1500–500BC). The torcs and jewelry are stunning, as are the crosses and croziers (AD600–1200) from Ireland's early Christian monasteries. Among the greatest gems here are the eighth-century Tara Brooch, the Ardagh Chalice and the Derrynaflan Hoard. Don't miss the rare Tully Lough Cross, an Irish altar cross of the eighth or ninth century. Found in fragments in Roscommon, it has been carefully recon-structed. The discovery of two Iron Age bog bodies in 2003 led to a radical new theory that linked them with sovereignty rituals, as the "Kingship and Sacrifice" exhibition explains.

History Upstairs, "Viking Ireland", spanning AD795–1170, documents invasions, trades and crafts and has scale models of Viking Dublin. "Medieval Ireland" covers life from the 12th century Anglo-Norman invasion to the Reformation. Further exhibitions feature items from Ancient Cyprus and Ancient Egypt.

THE BASICS

museum.ie
- H8
- Kildare Street
- 677 7444
- Tue–Sat 10–5, Sun 2–5
- Café
- Pearse
- Cross-city buses; Luas St. Stephen's Green
- Good (at ground level)
- Free
- Shop. Guided tours 45 minutes, small charge

HIGHLIGHTS

- Prehistoric gold
- Tara Brooch
- Ardagh Chalice
- Cross of Cong
- Tully Lough Cross
- Viking exhibition
- Egyptian room

TIP

- Many of the treasures of this museum are now on show at Collins Barracks (▷ 55).

St. Stephen's Green

HIGHLIGHTS

Newman University Church
- Marble panels
- Carved birds on capitals
- Ceiling
- Golden apse

This oasis of green in the city center was originally common land. Among notable structures around the green are Newman University Church and Fusiliers' Arch.

A public garden Ireland's famous Victorian park was formally opened to the public in 1880 thanks to the benevolence of Lord Ardilaun, a member of the Guinness family. The park's nine hectares (22 acres) retain the original layout, adorned with flowerbeds and crisscrossed with footpaths. Look out for the monuments and the public art—everything from a huge statue of a seated Lord Ardilaun to busts of James Joyce. In summer, free lunchtime concerts take place in the bandstand. The ornamental lake is home to waterfowl, including graceful swans and ducks, and there is a kids' playground.

Clockwise from top left: The Pagoda in St. Stephen's Green; St. Stephen's Green in colorful full bloom in the spring sunshine; Dubliners take to the lawns when the sun comes out

Newman University Church This tiny, ornate, Byzantine-style church is near the entrance to the Green. The church was opened in 1856, initially attached to the adjacent Catholic University and built by Cardinal Newman (canonized in October 2019) to promote his ideals. Inside, the Romanesque porch has four capitals that bear the symbols of many evangelistic and angelic figures. Above the main door is a richly decorated arch with an ornamental metal cross.

Fusiliers' Arch This monumental granite gate, known as Traitors' Arch, is a tribute to the soldiers of the Royal Dublin Fusiliers killed during the Boer War (1899–1902). On its northeast face are bullet marks thought to be from the 1916 Rising.

THE BASICS

Newman University Church
newman.nd.edu
➕ H8
✉ 87A St. Stephen's Green
☎ 475 9674
🕐 Mon–Sat 7.30–dusk, Sun 9.30–dusk. Church services: Mon–Fri 1.05, Sun 11 and 6.15
🚌 Cross-city buses; Luas St. Stephen's Green
🚆 Pearse
♿ None
🎟 Free

Fusiliers' Arch
➕ H8
✉ St. Stephen's Green
🚆 Pearse
🚌 Cross-city buses; Luas St. Stephen's Green

Trinity College

HIGHLIGHTS

● *Book of Kells*
● *Book of Durrow*
● *Book of Armagh*
● Science Gallery

TIPS

● The hugely popular *Book of Kells* is best visited early or come out of season.
● Regular walking tours (May–Oct) sheds light on the college's history. Check the front gate for information.

Stroll around the grounds of the famous college and visit the library, where you will find one of the most joyously decorative manuscripts of the first Christian millennium, the *Book of Kells*.

Surroundings An oasis of fresh air, Trinity College is also the noblest assemblage of classical buildings in the city. Inside, the open square is surrounded on three sides by some of Dublin's finest buildings—Paul Koralek's New Library (1978) to the south, Benjamin Woodward's splendidly carved Museum building (1853–55) to the east and Thomas Burgh's Old Library (1712–32) to the west. In 1857, Woodward altered Burgh's building and made its barrel-vaulted upper floor into a breathtaking space lined with books from floor to ceiling.

Clockwise from top left: Sphere within Sphere (1982–83) by Arnaldo Pomodoro, in the grounds of the college; Trinity College's famous Old Library, housing Ireland's largest collection of books and the Book of Kells; Trinity College, synonymous with learning in Dublin

Book of Kells The library is home to Ireland's greatest collection of medieval manuscripts. Among these, pride of place goes to the *Book of Kells* (*c*800), a Gospel book that has been bound in four separate sections so that its brilliantly ornamented pages and text may be viewed side by side. Displayed alongside are the important books of *Durrow* (*c*700) and *Armagh* (*c*800), the latter providing information about Ireland's patron saint, Patrick. The exhibition *Book of Kells* "Turning Darkness into Light" has excellent displays telling the history of illuminated manuscripts and books. The exit is through the amazing Long Room library.

Science Gallery This elegant gallery stages exhibitions and events which feature design, discovery and science.

THE BASICS

tcd.ie

✚ H7

✉ College Green

☎ 896 1000

🕐 Old Library Mon–Sat May–Sep 8.30–5, Sun 9.30–5; Oct–Apr 9.30–5, Sun 12–4.30. Campus daily

🚉 Pearse, Tara Street

🚌 Cross-city buses

♿ Good

🎫 Campus free; Library and *Book of Kells* expensive

❓ College tours May–Nov

More to See

DOUGLAS HYDE GALLERY

douglashydegallery.com

Part of the college's site, the contemporary gallery showcases talent from Ireland and overseas.
➕ H7 ✉ Trinity College, Nassau Street entrance ☎ 608 1116 🕐 Mon–Fri 11–6, Thu 11–7, Sat 11–5.30 🚉 Pearse 🚌 Cross-city buses 🚻 Few 👋 Free

GRAND CANAL

This pocket of the city has an atmosphere of calm but is also home to many of Dublin's most exciting cultural venues, such as the futuristic Bord Gáis Energy Theatre, which is surrounded by ultramodern apartments. From the dock here you can take a boat trip down the canal, or walk along it to Kilmainham.
➕ L7 (Grand Canal Docks) 🍴 Restaurants and cafés 🚉 Grand Canal Dock 🚌 2, 3

IRISH WHISKEY MUSEUM

irishwhiskeymuseum.ie

Learn about the history of Irish whiskey and its making with an engaging story-telling guide, who will lead you through scenes of the distillation process. There are also interactive films and theatrical sets taking you as far back as Roman times. It ends with a whiskey tasting experience.
➕ H7 ✉ 119 Grafton Street ☎ 525 0970 🕐 Daily 10–6 (last tour) 🚌 Cross-city buses; Luas St. Stephen's Green 🚻 Good 👋 Expensive

IVEAGH GARDENS

iveaghgardens.ie

One of Dublin's finest, yet least-known, parks was designed by Ninian Niven in 1865. The secluded gardens shelter a grotto, fountains, maze, sunken lawns, rockeries, wilderness and wood-lands. Exotic tree ferns and pre-1860s rose varieties in the Victorian Rosarium add to the romance of this place.
➕ H9 ✉ Clonmel Street ☎ 475 7816 🕐 Mon–Sat 8–6, Sun 10–6; closes at dusk in winter 🚌 Cross-city buses; Luas Harcourt 👋 Free

Slow travel on Dublin's Grand Canal

LEINSTER HOUSE

oireachtas.ie

Leinster House is the seat of the Irish government and home to the Dáil Éireann (House of Representatives) and Senead Éireann (Senate). It also contains a wonderful art collection. You can visit on a guided tour (Mon–Fri; email to book; photo ID required).

🔢 J8 ✉ Kildare Street ☎ 618 3781 🚉 Pearse 🚌 Cross-city buses; Luas St. Stephen's Green 🦽 Good 🎟 Free

MERRION SQUARE

Houses surrounding the best-preserved Georgian square in Dublin were home to Daniel O'Connell and William Butler Yeats, among others. The public park is a hidden gem, with well-maintained lawns and a statue of a reclining Oscar Wilde (▷ 76).

🔢 J8 🚉 Pearse 🚌 Cross-city buses 🎟 Free

NATIONAL LIBRARY

nli.ie

The library houses the world's largest collection of Irish documentary material. Research takes place in the reading room. Most popular are the Genealogy Advisory Service and family history research departments. There are also exhibitions.

🔢 J7 ✉ Kildare Street ☎ 603 0213 🕐 Mon–Wed 9.30–7.45, Thu–Fri 9.30–4.45, Sat 9.30–12.45 🍴 Café 🚉 Pearse 🚌 Cross-city buses; Luas St. Stephen's Green 🦽 Good 🎟 Free; reader's ticket required for info

NATURAL HISTORY MUSEUM

museum.ie

This branch of the National Museum has old glass cases and creaking floorboards, hardly changed since it was built in 1856. Inside is a skeleton of the giant Irish deer, and the upper floor is given over to animals of the world, including a massive skeleton of a whale.

🔢 J8 ✉ Merrion Street ☎ 677 7444 🕐 Tue–Sat 10–5, Sun 2–5 🚉 Pearse 🚌 Cross-city buses 🦽 Ground level access only 🎟 Free

OSCAR WILDE HOUSE

Wilde's family moved here in 1855 (it's now occupied by the American College of Dublin), and daily tours of the gracious Georgian town house give an insight into the great writer and the many scandals that surrounded his family.

🔢 J7 ✉ 1 Merrion Square ☎ 676 8939 🕐 Mon–Fri 2.30–5 🚌 Cross-city buses 🎟 Moderate

OSCAR WILDE STATUE

Danny Osborne's life-size sculpture of Wilde, at the northwest corner of Merrion Square, was unveiled in

An elegant door knocker, Merrion Square

1997 and depicts the writer, lying languidly on a huge piece of granite. It is created from naturally colored Irish stone.
✠ J7/8 ✉ Merrion Square 🚊 Pearse 🚌 Cross-city buses

RHA GALLAGHER GALLERY
rhagallery.ie
Within its five, well-lit gallery spaces, this large arts institution puts on high-profile exhibitions of Irish modern and contemporary art.
✠ H8 ✉ 15 Ely Place ☎ 661 2558 🕐 Mon–Sat 11–5, Wed 11–8, Sun 12–5 🚌 Cross-city buses

ST. ANN'S CHURCH
stann.dublin.anglican.org
Patronized by influential residents of Georgian Dublin, this 1720 church has a stunning neo-Romanesque facade. Seek out the Bread Shelf, part of a 300-year-old tradition of leaving out free bread for anyone who may be in need. Organ and choir concerts are held here.

✠ H7 ✉ Dawson Street ☎ 676 7727 🕐 Mon–Fri 10.45–2.45 (11–2 winter) and Sunday service 🚊 Pearse 🚌 Cross-city buses ♿ Good 🎟 Free

VIKING SPLASH TOURS
vikingsplash.ie
Take a guided journey through Viking Dublin on amphibious buses before splashing into the Grand Canal. It's great fun for kids.
✠ H8 ✉ St. Stephen's Green ☎ 707 6000 🕐 Feb to mid-Dec regular daily tours depart from St. Stephen's Green (tours last 90 minutes) 🎟 Expensive

WINDMILL LANE RECORDING STUDIOS
windmilllanerecording.com
Enter the world-famous studios that have produced albums by top names for 40 years. Guided by actual music producers, it offers insight into the technical wizardry behind the complex consoles.
✠ L7 ✉ 20 Ringsend Road ☎ 668 5567 🕐 Check for times; when not recording 🚉 DART: Grand Canal Dock 🎟 Expensive

Oscar Wilde statue in Merrion Square

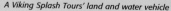

A Viking Splash Tours' land and water vehicle

Georgian Dublin Walk

Stroll back in time, passing some of the grandest Georgian buildings in Dublin. The squares provide a breath of fresh air in the city.

DISTANCE: 3km (2 miles) **ALLOW:** 2 hours plus stops

START

ST. STEPHEN'S GREEN NORTH
(▷ 70–71) 🔲 H8 🚌 Cross-city buses

1 Start at the north side of St. Stephen's Green (▷ 70–71), by the famous Shelbourne Hotel (▷ 112), close to Kildare Street. Walk down this street.

2 The National Museum (▷ 69) is on the right-hand side. It houses some of Ireland's greatest treasures. Continue along Kildare Street.

3 On your right you can see the grand buildings of Leinster House (▷ 75), the seat of the Irish government, and beyond, the National Library (▷ 75).

4 At the end of the street turn right into Clare Street, passing the Millennium Wing entrance of the National Gallery (▷ 68), to reach Merrion Square (▷ 75).

END

ST. STEPHEN'S GREEN SOUTH
(▷ 70–71) 🔲 H8 🚌 Cross-city buses

8 At the end of the street turn right onto Leeson Street Lower, and keep going until you reach the south edge of St. Stephen's Green.

7 Continue onto Fitzwilliam Street Upper to Fitzwilliam Square, and turn right along its southern edge. Some of the best Georgian houses are here—take a note of the doors and fanlights above. Turn left at the end of the square onto Pembroke Street Upper.

6 Walk along Merrion Square West and left into Merrion Square South. At the end is Number Twenty Nine, a gracious Georgian town house and museum (currently closed for major renovation). Turn right here.

5 Turn right here—across the road at No. 1, is Oscar Wilde's House.

Shopping

ALIAS TOM
aliastom.com
A longest-standing Dublin's men's store, Alias Tom has clothed many prominent Irish personalities, and stocks top labels for high-end tailoring and casual lines.
✚ H7 ✉ Duke Lane ☎ 671 5443
🚆 Pearse 🚌 Cross-city buses

ARAN SWEATER MARKET
aransweatermarket.com
Specialists in Aran sweaters, made in the tiny island community of Inis More since 1892, the store has a wide selection of top-quality woolens. Its wide selection includes everything from chunky men's sweaters to women's ponchos and coats. Look out for the vintage photos on the stairwell's walls.
✚ H7 ✉ Lower Grafton Street ☎ 064 662 3102 🚌 Cross-city buses

AVOCA
avoca.ie
Founded in 1723 and developed as a department store, this is one of Ireland's oldest surviving businesses. Its unique and exclusive high-quality items combine the traditional with the fashionable. The splendid food hall is packed with Irish delicacies, including preserves, oils and biscuits, all under the Avoca label. There's also a lovely café.
✚ H7 ✉ 11–13 Suffolk Street ☎ 677 4215
🚆 Pearse 🚌 Cross-city buses

BROWN THOMAS
brownthomas.com
Ireland's stylish department store showcases premium Irish and international designer clothes. You will also find household furnishings, cosmetics, leather goods, accessories and linens. There is a Restaurant on the third floor.
✚ H7 ✉ 88–95 Grafton Street ☎ 605 6666
🚆 Pearse 🚌 Cross-city buses

BUTLER'S CHOCOLATE CAFÉ
butlerschocolates.com
Come here to buy a mouthwatering selection of Irish chocolates, handmade using the original Mrs Bailey-Butler's recipe of 1932.
✚ H7 ✉ 51A Grafton Street ☎ 616 7004
🚆 Pearse 🚌 Cross-city buses

CELTIC WHISKEY SHOP
celticwhiskeyshop.com
This store sells a tempting selection of specialist whiskeys from Ireland and around the world—one of the city's best ranges—plus liqueurs and wines.
✚ H7 ✉ 27–28 Dawson Street ☎ 675 9744
🚆 Pearse 🚌 Cross-city buses

CHARLES BYRNE
charlesbyrne.com
Established in 1870, Charles Byrne is renowned for its expertise in stringed instruments, from mandolins to cellos. It also stocks Ireland's best range of *bodhráns* (traditional Gaelic drums), which are all handmade.
✚ G7 ✉ 21–22 Lower Stephen Street ☎ 478 1773 🚆 Pearse 🚌 Cross-city buses

---

MADE IN IRELAND

If you're looking for something of modern Ireland for your home, check out the following:
● Jerpoint Glass—heavy, hand-blown pieces of simple design with color bursts.
● Waterford Crystal—John Rocha's minimalist designer line has brought Waterford crystal bang up-to-date.
● Ceramics—look out for Nicholas Mosse's pottery and a range of great designs by Louis Mulcahy, one of Ireland's most prolific ceramicists.

CLEO

cleo-ltd.com

A bijou boutique for hand-knit sweaters, tweedy skirts and high-end country style. Run by the Joyce family since 1936, Cleo's specializes in natural-fiber clothes created in the knitters' and weavers' own homes.

🔢 H8 ✉️ 18 Kildare Street ☎️ 676 1421
🚉 Pearse 🚌 Cross-city buses

THE DESIGN TOWER

thedesigntower.com

A major restoration has turned this 19th-century sugar factory into seven floors of design studios. It's now home to independent artists and creators, such as fashion designer Róisín Gartland and sculptor Niamh Jackman.

🔢 J7 ✉️ Trinity Enterprise Centre, Pearse Street ☎️ 679 7272 🚉 DART Grand Canal Street 🚌 Cross-city buses

DESIGNYARD

designyard.ie

This space for crafts and decorative arts has a stunning jewelry gallery showcasing handcrafted pieces by Irish designers. Jewelry here is made with both precious and non-precious materials, and there are lovely glass and ceramics pieces too.

🔢 H7 ✉️ 25 South Frederick Street ☎️ 474 1011 🚉 Pearse 🚌 Cross-city buses

DUBRAY BOOKS

dubraybooks.ie

One of Dublin's largest independent booksellers, Dubray Books stocks an extensive collection of titles, including fiction, history and children's favorites sections, biographies and there's a large Irish history section.

🔢 H7 ✉️ 36 Grafton Street ☎️ 677 5568
🚌 Cross-city buses; Luas St. Stephen's Green

TRADITION LIVES ON

Irish traditional music is played in pubs all over the city every night of the week and is generally free. Music is often spontaneous, with musicians joining in an impromptu *seisún* (session). The Irish have grown up with this music; it has been handed down through the generations and instruments are often learned instinctively by watching others. All the traditional instruments and sheet music can be found in the excellent music shops across the city.

GALLERY 29

gallery29.ie

This Irish-owned store is the place to come for vintage posters—examples from the 1890s to 1990s include advertising posters for food, travel and arts—all of them original. The shop will also mount and frame them for you.

🔢 H7 ✉️ 29 Molesworth Street ☎️ 642 5784
🚉 Pearse 🚌 Cross-city buses

HODGES FIGGIS

waterstones.com/bookshops/hodges-figgis

Spread over an impressive four floors, this famous old bookstore was established in 1768 and is particularly revered for its extensive collection of works on Celtic and Irish history, culture, art and literature.

🔢 H7 ✉️ 56–58 Dawson Street ☎️ 677 4754
🚉 Pearse 🚌 Cross-city buses

HOUSE OF IRELAND

houseofireland.com

Browse traditional Irish fashion and exquisite pieces of Waterford Crystal, Belleek china and Aran knitwear plus lesser-known Galway Crystal in this new flagship store.

🔢 H7 ✉️ 114 Grafton Street ☎️ 671 1111
🚉 Pearse 🚌 Cross-city buses

WHAT'S YOUR STYLE?

There are some great shops in Dublin displaying a wide range of home interior products, many produced by Irish crafts-people and also by fashion designers turning to objects and furniture. Interior design is popular worldwide, and Dublin is gaining more shops for the enthusiast. Beautiful items in stone, wood, glass and other natural materials can be bought in both traditional and contemporary styles. You'll find items by Terence Conran, John Rocha and other well-known names.

JAMES FOX

jamesfox.ie

Established in 1881, this family-run specialist cigar and whiskey store stocks Ireland's largest selection of handmade Cuban cigars and rare Irish single malt whiskeys.

H7 ✉ 119 Grafton Street ☎ 677 0533
🚌 Cross-city buses; Luas St. Stephen's Green

JOHNSON'S COURT

An upscale collection of top-notch jewelry shops nestles in this small alley-way. Choose from a range of pieces, from luxury watches at Paul Sheeran to wedding rings at Donovan & Matson.

H7 ✉ Off Grafton Street 🚌 Cross-city buses; Luas St. Stephen's Green

JORGENSEN GALLERY

jorgensenfineart.com

Ireland's most popular fashion designer, Ib Jorgensen, turned to fine art in 1992 and hasn't looked back. Prepare to pay top prices for 19th- and 20th-century paintings and sculpture, and look out for solo exhibitions of international contemporary artists.

H7 ✉ 35 Molesworth Street ☎ 661 9721
🚆 Pearse 🚌 Cross-city buses

KERLIN GALLERY

kerlingallery.com

Established in 1988, this is one of Dublin's leading contemporary art galleries. It displays the work of top artists like Dorothy Cross, Aleana Egan, David Godbold and Sean Scully.

H7 ✉ Anne's Lane, off South Anne Street
☎ 670 9093 🚆 Pearse 🚌 Cross-city buses

KEVIN AND HOWLIN

kevinandhowlin.com

Shop here for hand-woven Donegal tweeds, made exclusively for the store. All the usual hardwearing items—jackets, waistcoats, hats and ties, in both modern and traditional styles—are of the highest quality.

H7 ✉ 31 Nassau Street ☎ 633 4576
🚆 Pearse 🚌 Cross-city buses

KILKENNY

kilkennyshop.com

This large emporium sells stylish Irish decorative objects such as Waterford Crystal, books, fashion and Celtic-inspired jewelry, with pieces from designers such as Orla Kiely. It has a café-restaurant overlooking Trinity College's grounds.

H7 ✉ 6–15 Nassau Street ☎ 677 7066
🚆 Pearse 🚌 Cross-city buses

LOUISE KENNEDY

louisekennedy.com

Kennedy's tasteful and exclusive ladies clothing and crystal collections are sold alongside elaborate accessories and gifts.

J8 ✉ 56 Merrion Square ☎ 662 0056
🚆 Pearse 🚌 Cross-city buses

ST. STEPHEN'S GREEN CENTRE

stephensgreen.com

A light, airy mall over three floors combines more expensive specialist

shops with Dunnes department store, bargain emporia and a food court.
🔲 H8 ✉ Corner of Grafton Street and St. Stephen's Green ☎ 478 0888 🚊 Pearse 🚌 Cross-city bus

SHERIDANS CHEESE SHOP

sheridanscheesemongers.com

This glorious shop is a wonderful outlet for Irish farmhouse varieties that are now winning awards worldwide. It also sells a range of Irish foods such as salmon and whiskey marmalades.
🔲 H8 ✉ 11 South Anne Street ☎ 679 3143 🚊 Pearse 🚌 Cross-city buses

SILVER SHOP

silvershopdublin.com

Admire the wide range of antique silver and silver-plate here, from the conventional to the unusual, such as Irish portrait miniatures. Prices start low and head up into the thousands of euros.
🔲 H7 ✉ 59 South William Street ☎ 679 4147 🚊 Pearse 🚌 Cross-city buses

STOCK DESIGN

pointy.com/shops/ireland/dublin/stock-design

This exciting store sells furniture, fabrics, rugs, lighting and an impressive range of fun and functional kitchen utensils and

---

IRELAND'S INTERNATIONAL DESIGNERS

Dublin fashion stores carry a great mix of contemporary, alternative and classic collections. Irish designers to look for include John Rocha, Paul Costelloe, Lainey Keogh, Daryl Kerrigan and Philip Treacy. Check out the handbags by Helen Cody and Orla Kiely, Vivienne Walsh's intricate jewelry, Pauric Sweeney's witty postmodern accessories stocked at Hobo, and Slim Barrett's quirky fairy-tale tiaras.

---

cookware. Serious cooks will jenjoy coming across more unusual items.
🔲 H8 ✉ 33–34 King Street South ☎ 679 4316 🚊 Pearse 🚌 Cross-city buses

SWENY'S PHARMACY

sweny.ie

Dating back to 1847 and described in detail in James Joyce's *Ulysses*, this store is no longer operating as a pharmacy. It now sells second-hand books and local crafts and is run by volunteers. Here, you can buy the famous lemon-scented soap that Leopold Bloom buys in the book.
🔲 J7 ✉ 1 Lincoln Place ☎ 083 457 9688 🚊 Pearse 🚌 Cross-city buses

TRINITY SWEATERS

sweatershop.com

The place to come for knitted Aran sweaters, Merino-wool ponchos, cashmere capes and Celtic scarves.
🔲 H7 ✉ 30 Nassau Street ☎ 671 2292 🚌 Cross-city buses; Luas St. Stephen's Green

ULYSSES RARE BOOKS

rarebooks.ie

Formerly known as Cathach Books, this is Dublin's leading rare and antiquarian bookshop, specializing in books of Irish interest, with a particular emphasis on 20th-century literature.
🔲 H7 ✉ 10 Duke Street ☎ 671 8676 🚊 Pearse 🚌 Cross-city buses

WEIR & SONS

weirandsons.ie

Founded in 1869, this family-run jewelry business is one of Grafton Street's oldest established stores. Look for top brands, including antique silver and luxury watches. Expect excellent service.
🔲 H7 ✉ 96–99 Grafton Street ☎ 677 9678 🚌 Cross-city buses; Luas St. Stephen's Green

Entertainment and Nightlife

BLEEDING HORSE

bleedinghorse.ie

This long-established bar on several levels, with a history dating back to 1649, is popular with locals and students especially at weekends when there is live music. There's decent pub food for lunch and dinner.

G9 24–25 Upper Camden Street 475 2705 Cross-city buses; Luas Harcourt

BORD GÁIS ENERGY THEATRE

bordgaisenergytheatre.ie

This striking, contemporary arts venue designed by Daniel Libeskind brings a 21st-century vibe to the rejuvenated Docklands area. It stages touring musical shows and big name music acts.

K7 Grand Canal Square 677 7999 Grand Canal Dock 1, 47, 56a, 77a

BRUXELLES

bruxelles.ie

Tucked away off Grafton Street, these three bars in one are best known for their live rock bands, plus regular DJ nights. There's a big screen showing major sports events, and a convivial saloon bar with a proud music heritage. There's a huge statue of Irish singer and songwriter Phil Lynott outside.

H7 7 Harry Street 677 5362 Cross-city buses; Luas St. Stephen's Green

RAISING A GLASS

The Irish have a reputation for enjoying a tipple and it's not surprising given the quality of their native drinks. For stout, sample Guinness or Murphy's. For whiskey— a traditional chaser to your stout—there's Jamesons or Bushmills, plus a growing number of regional single malt whiskies from local distillers.

CAFÉ EN SEINE

cafeenseine.ie

This opulent bar in two adjacent buildings has a French brasserie feel on three floors, with an indoor-outdoor "street garden" and retractable roof. It houses myriad food and drink outlets in one place.

H7 28 South Anne Street 677 4567 Pearse Cross-city buses

LA CAVE

lacavewinebar.com

This cozy basement wine bar in deep red has hundreds of wines on offer, including many by the glass. A long-standing local favourite, it also serves excellent French dishes.

H7 39 Dawson Street 679 4409 Cross-city buses

DOHENY AND NESBITT

dohenyandnesbitts.ie

This distinguished old pub attracts politicians and media people, as well as tourists and locals, to its three floors and well-stocked bars. Victorian-style mirrored walls and intimate snugs reflect its 19th-century origins. There's also a special Whiskey Corner.

J8 5 Lower Baggot Street 676 2945 10, 15X, 25X, 49X

GAIETY THEATRE

gaietytheatre.ie

An integral part of Dublin theaterland since it opened in 1871, this long-standing venue with its landmark Venetian facade, stages opera, musicals, classic plays, comedies, pantomime and touring shows. The Gaiety's agenda is ambitious—stop by to hear lunchtime arias during the opera season.

H8 South King Street 456 9569 Pearse Cross-city buses

THE HORSESHOE BAR

shelbournedining.ie

Over the decades, many a famous face has come to sit in the bar of the grand Shelbourne Hotel (▷ 112). Try a Dublin classic, Black Velvet, a cocktail made from Champagne and Guinness, and said to have been created here.

✚ H8 ✉ The Shelbourne Dublin, 27 St. Stephen's Green ☎ 663 4500

🚌 Cross-city buses; Luas St. Stephen's Green

KEHOE'S PUB

kehoesdublin.ie

A classic Dublin boozer, complete with mahogany fittings and stained-glass doors, Kehoe's has lost none of its Victorian charm. It hosts local stand-up comedians on Monday evenings.

✚ H7 ✉ 9 South Ann Street ☎ 677 8312

🚉 Pearse 🚌 Cross-city buses; Luas Dawson Street

INTERNATIONAL BAR

international-bar.com

Indulge in a hefty helping of Irish wit at the home of the Comedy Cellar, founded by Irish comic geniuses Ardal O'Hanlon, Dylan Moran and many others. The daily evening schedule of events includes stand-up and improv comedy, plus poetry, spoken word recitals and jazz.

✚ H7 ✉ 23 Wicklow Street ☎ 677 9250

🚉 Pearse 🚌 Cross-city buses

LOST LANE

lostlane.ie

Replacing former celeb favorite Lillie's Bordello, this is now a bijou live music venue hosting Irish musicians and DJ, often with free entry. It's open nightly until late.

✚ H7 ✉ Adam Court, Grafton Street ☎ 679 9204 🚉 Pearse 🚌 Cross-city buses

THE CLASSICS

Dublin has a thriving classical music and opera scene, though performances are irregular. The National Concert Hall stages a full schedule but other venues offer seasonal performances only. The Gaiety Theatre plays host to Dublin's most professional and prolific opera society. To find out about forthcoming events, call the box offices direct or check the listings in the *Irish Times*. Reservations are recommended for most of the performances.

MULLIGANS

mulligans.ie

A pub since 1820, Mulligans is a Guinness drinker's institution and has a long association with journalists and the Theatre Royal, opposite. This iconic place has had many famous visitors, including James Joyce and President J.F. Kennedy. Retaining its Victorian mahogany furnishings, it has resisted change and instead embraces its 19th-century heritage.

✚ H6 ✉ 8 Poolbeg Street ☎ 677 5582

🚉 Tara Street 🚌 Cross-city buses

NATIONAL CONCERT HALL

nch.ie

This busy Georgian concert hall has a modern 250-seat auditorium and is renowned for its world-class acoustics. It is home to the RTÉ National Symphony Orchestra and other Irish ensembles. Check for concerts—top artists perform here.

✚ H9 ✉ Earlsfort Terrace ☎ 417 0000

🚉 Pearse 🚌 14, 14A, 15A, 44, 74

O'DONOGHUE'S

odonoghues.ie

Renowned for its associations with the famous Irish folk group the Dubliners,

O'Donoghue's is a good place for nightly impromptu sessions of traditional music but it does get busy.
➕ J8 ✉ 15 Merrion Row ☎ 660 7194
🚆 Pearse 🚌 Cross-city buses

PERUKE & PERIWIG
peruke.ie
In a former wig-making store (hence the name), this cocktail bar harks back to 19th-century decadence, with its dark interior and plush velvet decor. There is a good choice of beers and spirits, and a whiskey menu, but it's the cocktails that are the appeal, complete with hand-made fruit syrups and made to unique recipes. Dinner is also served here.
➕ H8 ✉ 31 Dawson Street ☎ 672 7190
🚌 Cross-city buses; Luas St. Stephen's Green

THE SCHOOLHOUSE BAR
schoolhousehotel.com
Set in a lovely hotel converted from an old school in the leafy Ballsbridge neighborhood (▷ 111), this bar has many original features. Food is served all day, there's a large garden and live music Thursday through to Saturday.
➕ K8 ✉ 2–8 Northumberland Road
☎ 667 5014 🚆 Grand Canal Dock

THE SUGAR CLUB
thesugarclub.com
In a converted cinema, this multipurpose arts center with excellent acoustics, has regular live bands, DJ nights and occasional film screenings.
➕ H9 ✉ 8 Lower Leeson Street ☎ 678 7188 🚆 Pearse 🚌 10, 11, 14, 15, 44, 46, 86

Where to Eat

PRICES
Prices are approximate, based on a 3-course meal for one person.
€€€   over €50
€€   €30–€50
€   under €30

3FE (€)
3fe.com
One of a new breed of cool cafés in Dublin, 3FE boasts top roasts in a relaxed, rustic environment. It serves breakfast, brunch or lunch and you can even join a class (fee) to learn the best way to brew coffee.
➕ K8 ✉ 32 Grand Canal Street ☎ No phone ⏱ Mon 8–5, Sat–Sun 9–6 🚆 Grand Canal Dock 🚌 Cross-city buses

BANG RESTAURANT (€€–€€€)
bangrestaurant.com
Cool and minimal, Bang attracts a lively clientele, and its eclectic, modern European menu matches its chic interiors. It offers a five-course tasting menu.
➕ J8 ✉ 11 Merrion Row ☎ 400 4229
⏱ Lunch, dinner Mon–Sat 🚆 Pearse
🚌 Cross-city buses

BEWLEY'S CAFÉ (€)
bewleys.com
Steeped in tradition and nostalgia, Bewley's has been here since 1840. A major refurbishment in 2017 included the restoration of the building's fire-places and its stained-glass windows. This flagship branch of the famous

Bewley's chain promises to remain an iconic venue, with fairtrade coffee and a simple daytime menu.

➕ H7 ✉ 78 Grafton Street ☎ 672 7720
🕐 Mon–Wed 8am–10pm, Thu–Sat 8am–11pm, Sun 9am–10pm 🚉 Pearse 🚌 Cross-city buses

BREAD 41 (€)
breadnation.ie

Fans of home-baked sourdough bread should head here—an organic bakery and café with fresh sandwiches, pastries, seasonal jams and tangy pickles. There are also pizza options.

➕ J7 ✉ 41 Pearse Street ☎ 087 297 7284
🕐 Breakfast, lunch Mon–Sat 🚉 Pearse
🚌 Cross-city buses

CHILI CLUB (€€)
chiliclub.ie

This tiny, simple restaurant is loved for its fiery Thai curries, plus fresh stir-fried shrimp in ginger, pad Thai and tangy Thai soups.

➕ H7 ✉ 1 Anne's Lane, off Anne Street South
☎ 677 3721 🕐 Lunch Mon–Fri, dinner daily
🚉 Pearse 🚌 Cross-city buses

CORNUCOPIA (€)
cornucopia.ie

Wholefood and vegetarian dishes are served in a sunny dining room. Home-made dishes from breakfast through to dinner, with fresh salads, hot stews and delicious cakes, plus vegan dishes.

➕ H7 ✉ 19 Wicklow Street ☎ 677 7583
🕐 Breakfast, lunch and dinner Mon–Sat (Sun 12–9) 🚉 Pearse 🚌 Cross-city buses

DAX (€€€)
dax.ie

This renowned Irish-French restaurant operates in the intimate basement of a Georgian building. Its ever-changing seven-course menu may include Wicklow venison loin in red wine jus and sea bream with braised seaweed.

➕ J9 ✉ 23 Upper Pembroke Street ☎ 676 1494 🕐 Lunch Tue–Fri, dinner Tue–Sat
🚉 11, 11A, 46; Luas Harcourt

DIEP LE SHAKER (€€–€€€)
diep.net

Established nearly 20 years ago, this family-run business is as popular today as it was when it first opened. A stylish haunt, the restaurant offers very tasty, authentic and well-presented Thai cuisine, using local meat and fish.

➕ J8 ✉ 55 Pembroke Lane ☎ 661 1829
🕐 Lunch Tue–Fri, dinner Tue–Sat
🚉 Lansdowne Road 🚌 Cross-city buses

DUNNE & CRESCENZI (€€)
dunneandcrescenzi.com

This authentic Italian bistro has an extensive menu of specialties including slow-cooked Tuscan sausage. Enjoy the relaxed atmosphere, well-prepared food made with quality ingredients, and good Italian wines.

➕ H7 ✉ 14–16 South Frederick Street
☎ 675 9892 🕐 All-day dining 🚉 Pearse
🚌 Cross-city buses

> ### TIPS FOR EATING OUT
>
> ● Eating out is very popular in Dublin, so you will need to reserve ahead. Some restaurants close on Monday. Most upscale restaurants offer an excellent-value fixed-price lunch menu.
> ● Pre-theater or early-bird set menus are popular and good value. They are usually served until 7pm.
> ● A service charge of 12.5 percent may be added to your bill, especially if you are part of a group. If service is not included, a sum of 12.5–15 percent is the usual added tip.

L'ECRIVAIN (€€€)

lecrivain.com

Chef Derry Clarke's popular Michelin-starred Modern Irish restaurant continues to grow in stature. It is well known for its fresh fish, caught off the Irish coast, and its organic Irish meat.

➕ J8 ✉ 109a Lower Baggot Street
☎ 661 1919 🕐 Lunch Mon–Fri, dinner Mon–Sat 🚌 10

FIRE (€€€)

mansionhouse.ie

The spacious dining room is set in the resplendent belle époque-era Mansion House, built in 1715 to house the Mayor of Dublin. It offers a modern European menu with a twist. Jumbo tiger prawns from the wood-fired oven and prime steaks are the signature dishes. Pre-theater meals are good value.

➕ H8 ✉ The Mansion House, Dawson Street ☎ 676 7200 🕐 Dinner daily 🚌 Cross-city buses

THE GOTHAM CAFÉ (€–€€)

gothamcafe.ie

This lively, family-friendly café-restaurant is famed for its pizzas. Enjoy imaginative toppings, plus pasta and vegetarian dishes, huge salads and a kids' menu.

PUB GRUB

Pubs in Dublin are synonymous with drinking, Guinness, traditional Irish music and good *craic*. But pub food is popular and good value, particularly if you're on a tight budget. Expect to find hearty meals on the menu, including traditional Irish stews, the boxty (potato pancake) and colcannon (cabbage and potato). There is often a carvery offering a choice of meats and salads. Sample any of these accompanied by a pint of Guinness to be like a local.

Its walls are adorned with covers of *Rolling Stone* magazine.

➕ H7 ✉ 8 Anne Street South ☎ 679 5266
🕐 Lunch and dinner daily 🚌 Cross-city buses; Luas St. Stephen's Green

THE GREENHOUSE (€€€)

thegreenhouserestaurant.ie

This dining establishment, with a Michelin star, is sophistication without pretension. It has an interesting menu featuring contemporary European cuisine; enjoy its five or six-course "surprise tasting menu," showing off the Finnish chef Viljanen's exciting and inventive dishes.

➕ H8 ✉ Dawson Street, off St. Stephen's Green ☎ 676 7015 🕐 Lunch and dinner Tue–Sat 🚌 Cross-city buses; Luas St. Stephen's Green

HATCH & SONS IRISH KITCHEN (€–€€)

hatchandsons.co

A welcoming café-restaurant inside the interesting Little Museum of Dublin (▷ 66), Hatch & Sons celebrates fresh Irish ingredients. Traditional dishes include beef and Guinness stew, smoked fish platters and fresh sandwiches. The few craft beers make a good accompaniment.

➕ H8 ✉ 15 St. Stephen's Green ☎ 661 0075 🕐 Breakfast, lunch and early evening daily 🚌 Cross-city buses; Luas St. Stephen's Green

THE IVY (€€)

theivydublin.com

The Irish incarnation of the fashionable and hugely popular British restaurant offers an all-day menu from breakfast of eggs Benedict to steak tartare with whiskey. It's open late for food and cocktails (to 1.30am Fri and Sat).

H7 13–17 Dawson Street 695 0744
Breakfast, lunch, dinner daily Cross-city
buses; Luas Dawson Street

LANGKAWI (€€)

langkawi.ie

Excellent Malaysian restaurant with an
exciting, extensive menu reflecting the
influences of Chinese, Indian and Malay
cuisine. Specialties include spicy *kapitan*
and *gulai* curries, with seafood, meat
and vegetarian dishes.

K9 46 Upper Baggot Street 668
2760 Lunch Mon–Fri, dinner daily
Lansdowne Road 10

MARCO PIERRE WHITE STEAKHOUSE & GRILL (€€€)

marcopierrewhite.ie

This excellent restaurant specializes in
quality Irish ribeye, sirloin and fillet steak,
with a choice of classic sauces. Seafood
dishes include yellow fin tuna steaks.
There's a good-value early-bird menu.

H8 51 Dawson Street 677
1155 Lunch and dinner daily Pearse
Cross-city buses

OSTERIA LUCIO (€€)

osterialucio.com

In the new IT hub around the Grand
Canal, this Italian restaurant tucked in a
tunnel under a railway bridge embraces
industrial chic, wooden tables and rustic
exposed brick walls. However, the
cuisine is all about finesse, with
beautifully presented dishes.

K8 The Malting Tower, Clanwilliam
Terrace 6624 199 Lunch and dinner
Mon–Sat Pearse Cross-city buses

PEARL BRASSERIE (€€€)

pearl-brasserie.com

A real treat, Pearl is a classy restaurant
with romantic alcoves, an oyster bar,

modern art on the walls and a menu
that includes local fish and game dishes.

J8 20 Merrion Street Upper 661
3572 Lunch and dinner Mon–Sat
Pearse Cross-city buses

LA PENICHE (€€)

lapeniche.ie

La Peniche is on a barge, which at times
cruises the Dublin Canal, and at other
times stays moored up. Either way
it's a good alternative eating venue.
The French/Italian bistro-style food uses
simple local and organic produce with
excellent results. Fully licensed, it serves
French wines, beers and ciders.

J9 Grand Canal, Mespil Road 087
790 0077 (mobile) Dinner Wed–Sun
Grand Canal Dock 10, 10A, 18

THE PIG'S EAR (€€)

thepigsear.ie

In this upstairs restaurant overlooking
Trinity College, the renowned Irish chef
Stephen McAllister cooks contemporary
Irish food. It's an informal restaurant
offering good-value lunch and early
evening set menus.

H7 4 Nassau Street 670 3865
Lunch and dinner Mon–Sat Pearse
Cross-city buses

RESTAURANT PATRICK GUILBAUD (€€€)

restaurantpatrickguilbaud.ie

Expect superlative fine dining by French chef Guillaume Lebrun, with dishes of blue lobster and Wicklow lamb, and desserts to die for. The restaurant has a fine collection of Irish art.

J8 ⊠ 21 Upper Merrion Street ☎ 676 4192 Lunch and dinner Tue–Sat Pearse Cross-city buses

SABA (€€)

sabadublin.com

Serving first-class Thai and Vietnamese food using organic and Fairtrade ingredients, Saba (meaning "happy meeting place") is fun and stylish.

H7 ⊠ 26–28 Clarendon Street ☎ 679 2000 Lunch and dinner daily Pearse Cross-city buses

THE SADDLE ROOM (€€€)

marriott.co.uk

The refurbished Shelbourne Hotel (▷ 112) has produced a smart, steak and seafood restaurant. Dishes such as confit duck leg, roast venison and roast turbot use high-quality, locally sourced ingredients. The Oyster Bar, with its leather banquettes and intimate setting, occupies one side of the opulent fine dining room.

H8 ⊠ 27 St. Stephen's Green ☎ 663 4500 Breakfast, lunch and dinner daily Pearse Cross-city buses

SCIENCE GALLERY CAFÉ (€)

dublin.sciencegallery.com

This bright casual café lies inside the Science Gallery at Trinity College. It offers breakfast, hot sandwiches and stone-baked pizza, plus a bar.

J7 ⊠ Trinity College, Pearse Street ☎ 896 4091 Breakfast, lunch and early evening Mon–Fri, Sat–Sun from noon Pearse Cross-city buses

SHANAHAN'S ON THE GREEN (€€€)

shanahans.ie

A highly regarded American steak and seafood restaurant, Shanahan's is located in an elegant Georgian house. Enjoy top cuts of mature Angus steak, and choose from one of the 5,000 wines from the extensive cellar. Excellent service.

H8 ⊠ 119 St. Stephen's Green ☎ 407 0939 Lunch Friday; dinner Mon–Sat (Sun also in summer) Cross-city buses; Luas St. Stephen's Green

THE UNICORN RESTAURANT (€€–€€€)

theunicorn.restaurant

Understated elegance is the key to this Italian restaurant, established in 1938, and located in a quiet courtyard. Expect smart white tablecloths and a candlelit interior, with a select menu of *primi* and *secondi*, with good meat and fish dishes. There is an excellent wine selection.

J8 ⊠ 12b Merrion Court ☎ 662 4757 Lunch and dinner Mon–Sat Pearse Cross-city buses

WILD RESTAURANT (€€)

doylecollection.com

Located in the Westbury Hotel (▷ 112), this is the perfect place for afternoon tea, with great views of Grafton Street. Its regular menu features international dishes made from seasonal Irish ingredients.

H7 ⊠ Grafton Street ☎ 646 3352 Lunch and dinner daily (last meal orders 9.30pm Sun–Mon); afternoon tea 3pm–5.30pm Pearse Cross-city buses

Farther Afield

Just a short distance outside Dublin the beautiful Irish countryside is a delight, with pretty seaside villages, stunning lakes and ancient Celtic burial sites. A trip to the suburbs can also be rewarding.

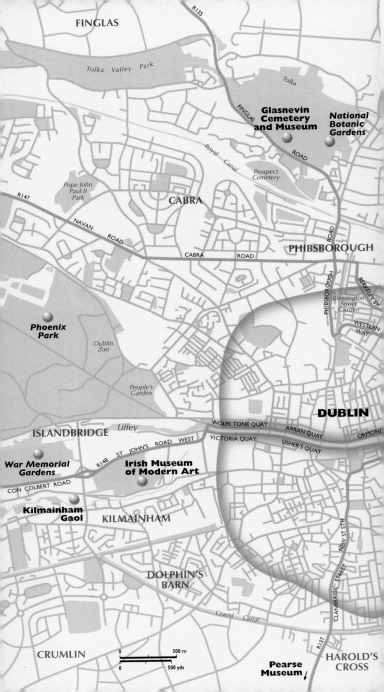

FINGLAS

R135

Tolka Valley Park

Tolka

FINGLAS

Glasnevin
Cemetery
and Museum

National
Botanic
Gardens

Royal Canal

ROAD

Prospect
Cemetery

Pope John
Paul II
Park

R147

CABRA

NAVAN ROAD

CABRA ROAD

PHIBSBOROUGH

PHIBSBOROUGH ROAD

BERKELEY ST

Blessington
Street
Garden

WESTERN WAY

Phoenix
Park

Dublin
Zoo

People's
Garden

DUBLIN

Liffey

ISLANDBRIDGE

WOLFE TONE QUAY

ARRAN QUAY

ORMOND

VICTORIA QUAY

USHER'S QUAY

R148 ST JOHN'S ROAD WEST

War Memorial
Gardens

Irish Museum
of Modern Art

CON COLBERT ROAD

Kilmainham
Gaol

KILMAINHAM

NEW ST STH

DOLPHIN'S
BARN

CLANBRASSIL STREET

Grand Canal

CRUMLIN

0   500 m

0   500 yds

R137

Pearse
Museum

HAROLD'S
CROSS

GAA Museum

Gaelic sports are celebrated here, and interactive games test wannabe players

THE BASICS

crokepark.ie/gaa-museum

☗ J3

✉ St. Joseph's Avenue

☎ 819 2323

🕐 Jun–Aug Mon–Sat 9.30–6, Sun 9.30–5; Sep–May Mon–Sat 9.30–5, Sun 10.30–5; adjusted schedule on match days

🚌 3, 11, 16, 41 from city center

💲 Expensive

HIGHLIGHTS

● Stadium tour
● Hall of Fame
● Ericsson Skyline
● Games Zone

Located in Croke Park, which is Ireland's most famous sporting venue, this is a place for every sports fan. The ground is the headquarters of the Gaelic Athletic Association (GAA), the country's largest sporting and cultural organization, with a long history.

Exhibits and tours The museum is dedicated to the history and culture of Ireland's national games, especially hurling, Gaelic football and shinty (a team game using a stick and ball, similar to hurling). The exhibition galleries, spread over two floors, include a Hall of Fame dedicated to Ireland's sporting heroes over the ages, plus a vast display of trophies. Dozens of audiovisual, interactive displays look back at the history of these sports from ancient times until today, highlighting their cultural impact on the country and the national identity. There is also an interactive Games Zone to test out your hurling and Gaelic football skills and reflexes. The Croke Park stadium tour, which must be booked separately, includes behind-the-scenes visits to the team dressing rooms, the media center and the players' tunnel—a thrilling experience, especially for sports enthusiasts.

Skyline tour The newest addition to this historic venue is the Ericsson Skyline tour, 17 levels high on the roof of the stadium. Visitors can walk over the rooftop and take in panoramic views of the city. The tour has a guide, but audio guides are available also.

Glasnevin Cemetery and Museum

Traditional stone Celtic crosses in the cemetery (left); The museum's glass exterior (right)

This enormous cemetery is a veritable Who's Who of modern Ireland's formative years: Charles Stewart Parnell, Michael Collins and Eamon de Valera are buried here, to name but a few.

Cemetery This is also the resting place of poet Gerard Manley Hopkins and writer Brendan Behan, as well as politician and engineer of Catholic Emancipation in Ireland, Daniel O'Connell (1775–1847), who founded the cemetery. Others buried here include thousands of suffragettes, artists and trailblazing women, not to mention the 1.5 million paupers who lie here in unmarked graves. The daily guided tours, led by local experts, show off some of the historic highlights of this Victorian burial ground, pointing out the most interesting headstones and carved Celtic crosses. Book ahead for tours, especially the one at 2.30pm when the famous speech delivered by republican Patrick Pearse in the cemetery in1915 is re-enacted by an actor.

The museum The new museum, located just inside the cemetery's main entrance, has permanent exhibitions, including "City of the Dead" depicting the cemetery's history. There's also a display on how grave robbers would steal corpses—the sturdy watchtowers were built to prevent such thefts. All the burial and cremation records, from the first burial in 1828 until today, are digitalized and visitors can access them in the genealogy section.

THE BASICS

glasnevintrust.ie

➕ E1/E2/F1

✉ Finglas Road, Glasnevin

☎ 882 6500

🕐 Mon–Sat 8.30–4.30, Sun 9–4.30

🚇 Drumcondra

🚌 140, 40 from O'Connell Street

♿ Good, except to crypt

🎟 Free; fee for tours

❓ Tours daily 11.30am and 2.30pm. Special tours daily Mar–Sep at 1pm; Sat–Sun Oct–Feb at 1pm

🍴 Tower Café

The Museum

glasnevinmuseum.ie

☎ 882 6550

🕐 Daily 10–5

✋ Moderate

HIGHLIGHTS

● Guided tours
● Michael Collins' plot
● Daniel O'Connell's crypt
● Permanent exhibition "City of the Dead"

FARTHER AFIELD TOP 25

93

Irish Museum of Modern Art

TOP 25

Exhibitions showcase a variety of art mediums; IMMA's exterior (right)

THE BASICS

imma.ie

+ C7

✉ Royal Hospital, Military Road, Kilmainham

☎ 612 9900

🕐 Tue–Sat 10–5.30 (Wed 10.30–5.30), Sun and public hols 12–5.30

🍴 Café

🚉 Heuston

🚌 26, 51, 51B, 78A, 79, 90, 123; Luas Heuston

♿ Good

✋ Free

❓ Free guided tours every afternoon. Well-stocked bookshop

HIGHLIGHTS

● Covered arcade
● Courtyard with sculptures
● Permanent collections
● Visiting exhibitions

The Royal Hospital at Kilmainham, once a haven for retired soldiers, is now an ultramodern cultural hub where regularly changing exhibitions showcase the latest trends in contemporary art.

Shelter The most important surviving 17th-century building in Ireland, the Royal Hospital at Kilmainham was founded as the Irish equivalent of the Invalides in Paris and the Chelsea pensioners' hospital in London. The architect, surveyor-general Sir William Robinson, laid the structure around an open quadrangle, and created a covered arcade around three sides of the ground floor where residents could stroll outdoors even in poor weather.

Transformation A hospital until 1927, the building was restored in 1984 and eventually opened as the Irish Museum of Modern Art in 1991. IMMA is Ireland's leading national institution for the collection and preservation of modern and contemporary works of art. The Permanent Collection of 1,650 works reflects trends in Irish and international art, including installations, video art, sculpture and paintings. The Madden Arnholz Collection comprises old master prints by innovative European print-makers such as Dürer, Rembrandt, Goya and Hogarth, together with books containing prints by Thomas Bewick and his family and one of Bewick's printing blocks. The museum stages changing exhibitions of modern art from Europe and beyond, and is renowned for its education.

Kilmainham Gaol

Leading figures in every rebellion against British rule since 1798 are associated with Kilmainham Gaol. For many Irish people, their imprisonment or death represents freedom through sacrifice.

Prisoners With its stark and severe interiors, Kilmainham has a fascination that is more inspirational than morbid. Opened in 1796, and altered frequently since, the gaol is made up of tall interlinked blocks in the middle, flanked by exercise and work yards. During its long history Kilmainham held civil and political prisoners, the earliest of whom were participants in the 1798 rebellion. The flow continued throughout the following century and included the "Young Ireland" rebels of 1848 (Europe's "Year of Revolution"), the Fenian suspects of 1867 and notable parliamentarians in the 1880s.

Conditions Overcrowding created appalling conditions when the Great Famine of 1845–49 drove many to petty crime. Closed in 1910, the gaol was reopened during the 1916 rebellion in Dublin to receive insurgents whose execution in the prison in the May and June of that year turned the tide of public opinion in many parts of Ireland in favor of the armed struggle. During the Civil War of the early 1920s, the gaol again housed anti-government rebels, including many women, and four Republican leaders were executed. The doors were finally closed in 1924. The gaol is now cared for by the state and has an excellent museum display.

THE BASICS

heritageireland.ie

➕ B7

✉ Inchicore Road, Kilmainham

☎ 453 5984

🕐 Apr–Sep daily 9.30–6; Oct–Mar Mon–Sat 9.30–5.30, Sun 10–6; last admission 1 hour before closing

🍴 Tea room

🚉 Heuston

🚌 51B, 78A, 79, 79A; Luas Suir Road

♿ Call in advance for wheelchair assistance

💷 Moderate

❓ Guided tours only. Prebook to avoid lines

HIGHLIGHTS

- East wing
- 1916 corridor with cells
- Museum display

TIP

- Ask the guide to shut you into one of the cells and find out what prison life was like.

Phoenix Park

Fallow deer roam the park (left); Ashtown Castle (middle); Dublin Zoo (right)

THE BASICS

phoenixpark.ie

➕ A3–6, B4–6, C5/6

✉ Parkgate Street

☎ 820 5800

🕐 Daily 24 hours

🚌 Cross-city buses; Luas Heuston

🍴 Café

♿ Moderate

✋ Free

Dublin Zoo

dublinzoo.ie

➕ B5

☎ 4748 900

🕐 Daily 9.30–5.30

✋ Expensive

HIGHLIGHTS

● Dublin Zoo
● Papal Cross
● Wild deer
● Áras an Uachtaráin

This vast green expanse near the heart of the city and enclosed by a 13km (8 mile) wall, is one of the largest urban parks in Europe. During its 350-year history it has been used for military maneuvers and as a sports ground. It is also the location of Dublin Zoo and of many stately homes.

History Phoenix Park started out as a royal deer park for King Charles II in 1662 (there deer roaming here still), but its history dates back further, with Neolithic remains including a burial mound and artifacts. In 1882, Lord Cavendish, the British chief secretary for Ireland, was murdered in the park. The Victorians built the People's Flower Gardens in the 19th century, including an ornamental lake.

The park today Established in 1831, Dublin Zoo is now home to rare species from around the globe in recreated natural habitats. Meet giraffes and zebra in the African Savannah, watch the penguins being fed, and see Asian lions. The zoo also has more than 2,000 plant species, from bamboo to Irish oak. The immense Papal Cross sits on the edge of an area known as the Fifteen Acres, built for Pope John Paul II's visit in 1979. There are occasional festivals and concerts held here, and energetic locals make good use of the bike hire facilities and running tracks. Áras an Uachtaráin, the official residence of the President of Ireland, is also in the park. There are tours of the residence on Saturday.

More to See

CASINO MARINO

casinomarino.ie

Guided tours show off this Mediterranean-inspired Casino, a compact, ingenious 18th-century creation. Its patron was James Caulfield, fourth Viscount Charlemont (1728–99), whose travels inspired the elegant design. Its floor plan is a Greek cross encircled by pillars on a raised podium, with lions at each corner creating a diagonal axis. The four state rooms boast curving wooden doors, stucco friezes and marquetry floors made from rare woods.

🚇 M1 ✉ Cherrymount Crescent, off Malahide Road, Marino ☎ 833 1618 🕐 Mar–Oct daily 10–5; last admission 45 mins before closing 🚌 Clontarf Road 🚌 14, 20A, 20B, 27A 🚹 Few 🎟 Inexpensive 🛈 Visit by guided tour only

JAMES JOYCE TOWER AND MUSEUM

joycetower.ie

Featured at the beginning of Joyce's *Ulysses*, this tower is one of many 19th-century Martello towers on Ireland's east coast and is prominent in the annual Bloomsday celebrations (▷ 114). The museum displays Joycean memorabilia. Even though Joyce only stayed here for six days, the tower is now the venue of a museum dedicated to his life and works. It was founded by local architect Michael Scott, who bought the tower in 1954.

🚏 See map ▷ 91 ✉ Sandycove Point, Glenageary ☎ 280 9265 🕐 Daily 10–6 in summer; 10–4 in winter 🚉 Dun Laoghaire 🚹 Few 🎟 Free

NATIONAL BOTANIC GARDENS

botanicgardens.ie

Founded in 1795, these huge gardens contain Ireland's most extensive and varied collection of plants. The curvilinear glasshouses, built by Richard Turner, a Dubliner who created a similar one for Kew Gardens in London, are among the finest surviving examples of 19th-century glass-and-iron construction. Many of the plants housed inside

Casino Marino

originate from southeast Asia.
Highlights include herbaceous
borders, alpines, roses, the rock
garden, pond and arboretum.

➕ F1 ✉ Glasnevin Hill Road ☎ 804 0300
🕐 Mar–Oct Mon–Fri 9–5, Sat–Sun and
public hols 10–6; Nov–Feb Mon–Fri
9–4.30, Sat–Sun and public hols 10–4.30
🚂 Drumcondra 🚌 4, 9 ♿ Good except for
some glasshouses 💶 Free; fee for parking

NATIONAL TRANSPORT MUSEUM

nationaltransportmuseum.org

Located at the Heritage Depot,
this museum houses a selection of
historic vehicles from Ireland,
including century-old trams and an
1883 Merryweather fire appliance.
A fleet of military vehicles includes
several World War II classics. There
are also handcarts that were
attached to horses and used to
transport goods.

➕ See map ▷ 91 ✉ Heritage Depot,
Howth Demesne ☎ 832 0427 🕐 Sat–
Sun and public hols 2–5 🚂 Howth
💶 Inexpensive

PEARSE MUSEUM

pearsemuseum.ie

This former school was run by
Patrick Pearse, the Dublin-born poet
and revolutionary executed in 1916
at Kilmainham Gaol (▷ 95). It has
a nature study room displaying
Irish fauna and flora. The museum
is set in the attractive St. Enda's
Park, which is said to have inspired
his writing.

➕ See map ▷ 90 ✉ St. Enda's Park,
Grange Road, Rathfarnham ☎ 493 4208
🕐 Mar–Oct Mon–Sat 9.30–5.30; Nov–Jan
9.30–4; Feb 9.30–5; Sun and public hols from
10 🚌 16 🍴 Café ♿ Few 💶 Free

WAR MEMORIAL GARDENS

heritageireland.ie

These gardens, including a sunken
rose garden, designed by Sir Edwin
Lutyens, are dedicated to the
49,400 Irish soldiers who died in
WWI, with thousands of names
etched in the granite book rooms.

➕ A7 ✉ Islandbridge ☎ 475 7816
🕐 Mon–Fri 8–dusk, Sat–Sun 10–dusk
🚌 51, 68, 69 💶 Free

Golden harp at the War Memorial Gardens

Dublin from the DART

VIEWS FROM THE DART

- Dalkey Island off Killiney
- Sailboats off Dun Laoghaire
- Blackrock's public park and private gardens
- Wetlands bird sanctuary at Booterstown
- Custom House between Tara Street and Connolly Station
- Urban jungle of Kilbarrack, backdrop for novels *The Commitments*, *The Snapper* and *The Van*, Roddy Doyle's prize-winning trilogy

BRAY

This attractive seaside town, out toward the southern end of the DART line, has long been a popular holiday resort enjoyed for its sandy beach and mile-long promenade. The Jazz Festival in May and summer events attract the crowds. There are well-marked walks and great views around nearby Bray Head.

DUN LAOGHAIRE

Invigorating walks along the piers at Dun Laoghaire, a Victorian seaside resort once known as Kingstown, are something of a Dublin institution. The scenery is stunning, and you can see the ferries plying across the Irish Sea. A lighthouse marks the end of the East Pier, while the West Pier attracts fishing enthusiasts. There are good seafood restaurants here, and the National Maritime Museum of Ireland.

HOWTH

This promontory to the north of Dublin is a traditional fishing village and fashionable suburb. A popular sailing hub, the marina is always packed with yachts from Ireland and farther afield. Howth DART station is near the harbor and close to all the waterside activity, bars and restaurants.

Fishing boats in the harbor at Howth

Howth coastal path

DART DUBLIN AREA RAPID TRANSIT

KILLINEY & DALKEY

The resort of Killiney is known affectionately as Dublin's Riviera. Take a walk along the Vico Road for what is arguably the most breathtaking view in Dublin. Look out to Dalkey Island, a craggy piece of land captured by the Vikings and later the site of Christian communities. In summer, fishermen in nearby Coliemore Harbour run boat trips so visitors can see the resident goats, the ruined oratory and the Martello tower.

SANDYCOVE

The popular village of Sandycove is famous for its seaside promenade, which runs north to Dun Laoghaire. It is named after a small cove near the rocky point on which a Martello tower was built during the Napoleonic Wars. James Joyce chose the Martello tower along the waterfront as the setting for the first chapter of *Ulysses,* and the museum inside displays much Joycean memorabilia. It forms part of the annual Bloomsday festival on June 16th, which celebrates the hero of *Ulysses*. The day brings many Joycean fans dressed in period costume to Sandycove. A bracing swim in the sea may introduce you to brave locals who plunge into the ocean at the Forty Foot promontory all year around.

DALKEY

Travel only a few stops south on the DART and you'll find yourself in the attractive former fishing village of Dalkey, well known for its literary associations. George Bernard Shaw lived in the village and James Joyce set chapter two of *Ulysses* here. The Heritage Centre is accessed through Goat Castle in Castle Street. From the battlements there is a splendid view of the sea and mountains. Good pubs and restaurants enhance a visit.

View from Dalkey Hill across Killiney Bay toward the distant Wicklow hills

FARTHER AFIELD **DUBLIN FROM THE DART**

Excursions

THE BASICS

heritageireland.ie
Distance: 50km (31 miles)
Journey Time: 1 hour 30 mins
✉ Brú Na Bóinne Visitor Centre, Donore, Co Meath
☎ 041 988 0300
🕐 Jun–Sep daily 9–7; Oct, Feb-Apr 9.30–3.30; May 9–4.30; Nov–Jan 9–3
🚌 Bus Éireann 100 to Drogheda, then 163 to Donore village (10-min walk). Also bus tours

BRÚ NA BÓINNE

A designated UNESCO World Heritage Site, Brú Na Bóinne is one of the most important prehistoric monuments in Europe. "The Palace of the Boyne" is the name given to a large group of neolithic remains in the central Boyne Valley, 11km (7 miles) west of Drogheda and 50km (31 miles) northwest of Dublin. The huge, white-fronted Newgrange is the best known, a 5,200-year-old passage tomb leading to a chamber with three alcoves. The nearby mound of Knowth (northwest) was of similar importance historically. There are restrictions to visits here. The great tombs can be seen only with a guided tour and in small groups leaving from the visitor center (booking ahead is advisable).

THE BASICS

glendalough.ie
Distance: 48km (30 miles)
Journey Time: 1 hour 15 mins
☎ 404 45325
🕐 Visitor center mid-Mar to mid-Oct daily 9.30–6; mid-Oct to mid-Mar 9.30–5; last admission 45 mins before closing
🚌 St. Kevin's bus from Bray and Dublin. Can also be reached on coach tours from Dublin. The most direct route if driving is the N11 (M11) south

GLENDALOUGH

Glendalough ("valley of two lakes") was one of Ireland's most venerated monastic sites. Its spectacular setting makes it one of eastern Ireland's premier attractions, lying 48km (31 miles) south of Dublin. Situated at the end of a long valley stretching deep into the Wicklow Mountains, Glendalough grew up around the tomb of its founder, St. Kevin. He was abbot until his death in AD618 and this early Christian monastery became famous throughout Europe as a seat of learning. The core of the old monastery consists of a roofless cathedral (c900), a well-preserved Round Tower (30m/98ft high) and St. Kevin's Church, roofed with stone and with a 12th-century round-tower belfry. Over-looking the Upper Lake is another enchanting church called Reefert. There are good walks in the woods and it can get very busy in high summer. The visitor center also acts as an information outlet for the Wicklow Mountains National Park.

MALAHIDE CASTLE

In the pretty seaside town of Malahide, this stunning castle, set on 250 acres of parkland, stayed mainly in the hands of the Talbot family from 1185 until 1973. The core of the castle is a medieval tower, and in the adjoining banqueting hall the walls are hung with magnificent Irish portraits. Most of the period furnishings are from the Georgian era. Enjoy a tour of the castle rooms, including the Oak Room. Also explore the walled gardens at your own pace. The beautiful Talbot Botanic Gardens were mainly created by Lord Milo Talbot in the mid-20th century. There is also an Avoca gift shop and café (▷ panel, 106), plus the visitor center in the courtyard.

THE BASICS

malahidecastleandgardens.ie
Distance: 13km (8 miles)
Journey Time: 45 mins
☎ 846 2184
🕐 Daily 9.30–4.30 (last tour); Nov–Mar 9.30–3.30. Guided tours every hour
🚌 42
🚆 From Connolly Station to Malahide, then a 10-min walk

POWERSCOURT

Beautifully set in the heart of the wild Wicklow Mountains, an hour away from Dublin, this house is renowned for its magnificent Italianate gardens. Careful restoration has converted the 18th-century Palladian mansion into an excellent Avoca store (▷ panel, 106) with a terrace café. The setting is made more dramatic by with the cone-shaped Sugar Loaf mountain in the distance. To the south, the house looks out over magnificent stepped terraces, with ornamental sculpture and a statue throwing a jet of water high in the air. Gardens stretch to either side; the one to the east is Japanese, the other walled, with wrought-iron gates. There is also a huge pet cemetery. The story goes that when the designer of the terraces, Daniel Robertson inspected the work every morning, he was pushed around in a wheelbarrow, swigging sherry. The waterfall is a short drive (5km/3 miles) away and is the highest waterfall in Ireland (there is an additional entrance fee to pay).

THE BASICS

powerscourt.ie
Distance: 19km (12 miles)
Journey Time: 1 hour
☎ 204 6000
🕐 Daily 9.30–5.30 (gardens close at dusk in winter)
🚌 44 to Enniskerry, then walk
🚆 DART to Bray, then 185 feeder bus to Enniskerry
❓ Waterfall inadvisable to reach on foot as the footpath is incomplete

Shopping

BLACKROCK MARKET

blackrockmarket.com

Bargain hunters flock to Blackrock, 8km (5 miles) south of Dublin, for the lively market held every Saturday. Stalls sell clothes, bric-a-brac, fine art, crafts and antiques. There are usually around 50 traders, plus a wide range of refreshment stands.

➕ Off map ✉ Blackrock ☎ 283 3522
🚆 Blackrock 🚌 G7, 7A, 8, 17

DUNDRUM TOWN CENTRE

dundrum.ie

A 22-minute ride away on the Luas, this large, modern shopping venue has more than 120 stores, with big names such as Harvey Nichols, House of Fraser and Hamleys. Spend the day here—it also has restaurants, cafés and a multiplex cinema.

➕ Off map ✉ Sandyford Road, Dundrum
☎ 299 1700 🚌 17, 14A; Luas Sandyford

LIFFEY VALLEY SHOPPING CENTRE

liffeyvalley.ie

A 20-minute drive southwest of Dublin, with more than 90 retail outlets, including Tommy Hilfiger and Diesel.

➕ Off map ✉ Fonthill Road, Clontalkin
🚌 25, 66, 78A

NAUGHTON BOOKSELLERS

naughtonsbooks.com

Browse this family-run bookstore crammed with thousands of antiquarian and rare books.

➕ Off map ✉ 8 Marine Terrace, Dun Laoghaire ☎ 280 4392 🚆 Dun Laoghaire, Sandycove, Glasthule

PEOPLE'S PARK MARKET

The Sunday food market here (11–4) sells hot baked goods and artisan foods.

➕ Off map ✉ People's Park, Dun Laoghaire
🚆 DART Dun Laoghaire

Entertainment and Nightlife

THE ABBEY TAVERN

abbeytavern.ie

A famous Howth venue, this 16th-century traditional pub comes complete with flagged floors and open fires. There is traditional music and dancing, plus good food.

➕ Off map ✉ 28 Abbey Street, Howth
☎ 839 0307 🚆 Howth

CIVIC THEATRE

civictheatre.ie

A community arts venue in the south-west suburbs providing drama, dance, opera and classical music.

➕ Off map ✉ Blessington Road, off Belguard Square East, Tallaght ☎ 462 7477 🚌 49, 50, 54A, 65, 77; Luas Tallaght

GAELIC GAMES

gaa.ie; crokepark.ie

Traditional Gaelic football and hurling are fast, physical sports, and the All-Ireland finals are played before huge crowds at Croke Park (▷ 92) in early and late September. These matches are popular and tickets sell out very quickly so you'll need to plan ahead.

➕ J3 ✉ Croke Park Stadium, St. Joseph's Avenue ☎ 819 2300 🚌 11, 16, 51A

THE HELIX
thehelix.ie
This modern arts complex at the City University has three auditoria and serves a mixed program of classical concerts, drama and ballet, plus rock and pop music.
🔲 Off map ⊠ Dublin City University, Collins Avenue, Glasnevin ☎ 700 7000 🚌 4, 11, 13, 16, 44

HORSE RACING
leopardstown.com
Leopardstown Race Course is one of Ireland's busiest. It hosts the Irish Gold Cup and a traditional post-Christmas festival, among other events.
🔲 Off map ⊠ Leopardstown ☎ 289 0500 🚊 Luas Sandyford

JOHN KAVANAGH
Adjacent to Glasnevin Cemetery, this cozy family pub is known by locals as the Gravediggers. Apparently it was where workers would head for a pint after completing their duties. Little has changed inside since it opened in 1833. It serves good, home-cooked food.
🔲 G1 ⊠ 1 Prospect Square ☎ 830 7978 🚌 13, 19, 40

JOHNNIE FOX'S
jfp.ie
This is popular with visitors from near and far, for its turf fires, live music, hooley dancing and tasty seafood. If you want to eat, reserve ahead.
🔲 Off map ⊠ Glencullen ☎ 295 5647 🚌 Special express bus—reservations advisable (☎ 822 1122, expressbus.ie)

RUGBY
avivastadium.ie; irishrugby.ie
Ireland's fans are always enthusiastic when it comes to their national team. Details of fixtures for local clubs, like Bective Rangers and Wesley, are published in the local press. The slick Aviva Stadium is the home of Ireland's national rugby team. The annual Six Nations tournament sees at least one match take place here in February to March.
🔲 M9 ⊠ Aviva Lansdowne Road Stadium, Ballsbridge ☎ 647 3800 🚉 Lansdowne Road 🚌 5, 7, 7A, 45

SOCCER
fai.ie; tallaghtstadium.ie
The Irish have become soccer fanatics in recent years, and Dublin pauses when the national team plays. The domestic season runs from March to November. You can buy tickets for matches involving Ireland's most successful team, Shamrock Rovers (at Tallaght Stadium) at the gate.
🔲 Off map ⊠ Tallaght Stadium, Whitestown Way ☎ 460 5948 🚌 49, 65; Luas Tallaght

STELLA CINEMA RATHMINES
stellacinemas.ie
For more than just a regular movie night experience, this art deco independent movie theater, recently refurbished to retain all that 1920s glamor, has welcoming armchairs, cozy sofas and a cocktail bar.
🔲 Off map ⊠ 207–209 Rathmines Road Lower ☎ 44967 014 🚌 14, 15, 65, 83

GOLF
The growth in the number of championship golf courses in Dublin is staggering. Many clubs welcome non-members, and fees are reasonable. The most famous are Portmarnock (▷ 111) and Royal Dublin; also try Castle and Grange, Hermitage and Island.

Where to Eat

PRICES

Prices are approximate, based on a 3-course meal for one person.

€€€ over €50
€€ €30–€50
€ under €30

AQUA (€€–€€€)

aqua.ie

Aqua wins top prize for its spectacular location, at the end of the pier, overlooking the sea. It's known for its excellent seafood, such as Howth grilled lobster, with fresh fish caught locally, plus some Irish game dishes. Excellent service.

🔼 Off map 🖂 1 West Pier, Howth 🕾 832 0690 🕐 Lunch and dinner Tue–Sun 🚊 Howth

AVOCA SALT (€)

avoca.com

This bright and airy café is attached to the fabulous Food Market. The menu is globally influenced using local produce, from Persian lamb casserole to Wicklow venison.

🔼 Off map 🖂 11A The Crescent, Monkstown 🕾 202 0230 🕐 Breakfast, lunch and dinner daily 🚊 Monkstown

CAVISTONS (€€)

cavistons.com

This highly regarded seafood restaurant creates dishes with global influences using the freshest ingredients.

🔼 Off map 🖂 59 Glasthule Road, Sandycove 🕾 280 9245 🕐 Lunch Tue–Sat, dinner Thu–Sat (6–8pm) 🚊 Sandycove and Glasthule 🚌 59

HARTLEY'S (€€–€€€)

hartleys.ie

Dine on fish, prime steak and seafood at this Victorian former railway station overlooking the harbor. In fine weather, tables are set up on the outside terrace.

🔼 Off map 🖂 1 Harbour Road, Dun Laoghaire 🕾 280 6767 🕐 Lunch and dinner Tue–Sun 🚊 Dun Laoghaire 🚌 7

KING SITRIC (€€€)

kingsitric.ie

The fish are landed a few yards from Dublin's famous seafood restaurant, named after the city's 11th-century Norse king. Going strong for more than 40 years, it has an outstanding menu and wine cellar. The more casual East Café (€€) Bar is on the same site.

🔼 Off map 🖂 East Pier, Howth 🕾 832 5235 🕐 Restaurant: dinner Wed–Sat, lunch Sun. Cafe: lunch and dinner daily 🚊 Howth 🚌 31, 31B

TOSCANA (€€)

toscana.ie

Authentic Italian dishes are created using organic local meat, fish and vegetables from their Wicklow farm. There's a stunning sea view and a good weeknd brunch menu.

🔼 Off map 🖂 5 Windsor Terrace 🕾 230 0890 🕐 Daily lunch and dinner 🚊 DART Dun Laoghaire

AVOCA CAFÉS

The Avoca Handweavers were founded in 1723, and in recent years their award-winning cafés have been the topic of conversation about as much as their famous shops. You can find branches in the village of Avoca, the home of the original mill, at Kilmacanoge near Bray, at Powerscourt House (▷ 103) and in Suffolk Street, Dublin. Homemade is the key word and the delicious desserts are especially noteworthy, along with great scones, cookies and cakes.

From boutique hotels to elegant Georgian town houses, there are some great choices when deciding where to stay in Dublin. North of the river Liffey, staying in a bed-and-breakfast is a less-expensive option.

Introduction

As you'd expect from a lively, modern and cosmopolitan capital, Dublin offers every type and style of place to stay. There is a huge choice, from budget hotels and self-catering to good-value Georgian town houses converted into charming hotels or guesthouses, fashionable boutique hotels and luxury 5-star establishments. Don't be afraid to choose a place in the suburbs; room rates are lower and the city's public transportation system is efficient.

Accommodations Options

Exclusive hotels in the heart of the city, in particular around St. Stephen's Green and Merrion Square, offer high standards and prices to match. For decent quality and value, try the town house hotels or stay in the quieter suburbs such as leafy Ballsbridge (Dublin 4), known as the embassy area. A short bus ride or 15-minute walk into town, it is also convenient for the Aviva Stadium, 3Arena, Docklands and financial center.

Reservation Advice

Many visitors make their accommodations reservations online, and it is useful to compare several websites, including that of the hotel itself. During special events like rugby and soccer internationals and St. Patrick's Day, the city gets very busy, and hotel rates rise accordingly—book as far ahead as possible. Prices sometimes include a full Irish breakfast, but many places now offer room-only rates. If you have not booked in advance, Dublin Tourism in Suffolk Street offers an on-the-spot booking service, for Dublin and the whole of Ireland.

SELF-CATERING

Most self-catering options are in the suburbs or on the coast, but there are some in the city. Check out visitdublin.com, which is a good place to start your search for whatever style of accommodations you are seeking.

Wherever you want to base yourself in Dublin there is a choice of accommodations to suit your style and your budget

Budget Hotels

ARIEL HOUSE

ariel-house.net

Occupying two gracious Victorian town houses in a peaceful suburb, near Aviva Stadium, this hotel has good standard guest rooms. It's known for its home-made Irish breakfasts and good service.

🔋 L9 ✉ 50–54 Lansdowne Road, Ballsbridge ☎ 668 5512 🚆 Lansdowne Road 🚌 7, 45

CASSIDY'S HOTEL

cassidyshotel.com

This 119-room hotel at the northern end of O'Connell Street, offers 4-bed family rooms. Grooms Bar and Bistro are an added bonus. The executive wing has a fitness suite.

🔋 H5 ✉ 6–8 Cavendish Row, O'Connell Street Upper ☎ 878 0555 🚌 Cross-city buses

CLAYTON HOTEL BALLSBRIDGE

claytonhotelballsbridge.com

The building of this good-value hotel in Ballsbridge, formerly Bewley's Hotel, is a former 19th-century Masonic school. Rooms are bright and spacious, with gardens, and there are family rooms available and car parking. It is close to the RDS, a 20-minute walk to the city center, and the Aircoach stops outside.

🔋 Off map ✉ Merrion Road ☎ 668 1111 🚌 4, 7

HARCOURT HOTEL

harcourthotel.ie

Incorporating eight Georgian listed buildings, including George Bernard Shaw's former home, this is in a lively location and has an on-site nightclub.

In addition to standard doubles, some rooms sleep up to five people.

🔋 G9 ✉ 60 Harcourt Street ☎ 478 3677 🚌 Cross-city buses

HOUSE DUBLIN

housedublin.ie

This neat little boutique guesthouse has quirky features in the guest rooms, a bright conservatory and a gin room. There's also a relaxing courtyard.

🔋 H9 ✉ 27 Lower Leeson Street ☎ 905 9090 🚌 Cross-city buses

THE LEESON LODGE

leesonbridgehouse.ie

In a Georgian town house, this good-value guesthouse is a short walk from the city center, in a quiet spot over-looking Grand Canal. Some double rooms offer a jet bath.

🔋 J9 ✉ 1 Upper Leeson Street ☎ 668 1000 🚌 Cross-city buses; Luas: Sandyford

MALDRON HOTEL SMITHFIELD

maldronhotelsmithfield.com

This good-value hotel in the heart of Smithfield is close to the famous music pub The Cobblestone (▷ 60), and close to the Luas stop. The rooms here are cheerful, some with a balcony, and have views of the city center.

🔋 F6 ✉ Smithfield ☎ 485 0900 🚌 Luas Smithfield

TRINITY COLLEGE

tcd.ie

From late May to mid-September, you can rent student rooms in 400-year-old Trinity College. Most of the apartments have three to four bedrooms, a small kitchen, living room and bathroom. The location is superb.

🔋 H7 ✉ College Green ☎ 896 4477 🚆 Pearse, Tara Street 🚌 Cross-city buses

Mid-Range Hotels

BROOKS HOTEL
brookshotel.ie
Guest rooms here are furnished with Irish wooden furniture. Its Jasmine Bar hosts special whiskey tasting events, and guests can use the residents' lounge and gym.

G7 ⊠ Drury Street ☎ 670 4000
🚌 Cross-city buses; Luas St. Stephen's Green

BUSWELLS
buswells.ie
Comprising 67 guest rooms in five grandiose Georgian town houses, Buswells is one of Dublin's oldest hotels. This bar is a popular spot for MPs from the Dáil, opposite.

H7 ⊠ 23–27 Molesworth Street ☎ 614 6500 🚆 Pearse 🚌 Cross-city buses

DEER PARK HOTEL GOLF & SPA
deerpark-hotel.ie
Only 14km (8.5 miles) from central Dublin, this hotel is located on a quiet hillside in the grounds of Howth Castle, overlooking the sea. It has a large golf complex and spa.

Off map ⊠ Howth ☎ 832 2624
🚆 Howth

GRAND CANAL HOTEL
grandcanalhotel.ie
This contemporary hotel with 142 rooms is well located for visiting the 3Arena, RDS and Aviva Stadium. Extras in each room include a laptop safe and a coffee machine.

L8 ⊠ Upper Grand Canal Street ☎ 646 1000 🚆 Grand Canal Dock 🚌 5, 7, 7A, 8, 18, 27X, 45

HARRINGTON HALL
harringtonhall.com
This beautiful Georgian guesthouse has genteel public areas and generously proportioned guest rooms. A few free car parking spaces are available.

G9 ⊠ 70 Harcourt Street ☎ 475 3497
🚌 Cross-city buses

HERBERT PARK HOTEL
herbertparkhotel.ie
Enjoy quiet comfort in this bright and airy hotel in Dublin's exclusive residential neighborhood. Many of the 153 rooms overlook the peaceful Herbert Park.

Off map ⊠ Herbert Park, Ballsbridge
☎ 667 2200 🚆 Lansdowne Road 🚌 7, 45

IVEAGH GARDEN HOTEL
iveaghgardenhotel.ie
Europe's first sustainable hotel generates its own electricity from an underground river. The 145 guest rooms have huge windows and marble bathrooms.

G9 ⊠ 72–74 Harcourt Street Upper
☎ 568 5500 🚌 Cross-city buses

JURY'S INN CHRISTCHURCH
jurysinns.com
Opposite Christ Church Cathedral, the 182 modern guest rooms here are a good size. There are some family rooms and spacious executive rooms.

K7 ⊠ Christchurch Place ☎ 454 0000
🚌 Cross-city buses

MERLIN HOTEL
marlinhotel.ie
This brand-new hotel is slick and bright. Its rooms vary in size but all have huge comfortable beds and TV screens. The lobby is a laid-back area with plenty of sofas and laptop plug-in points.

G8 ⊠ 11 Bow Lane East ☎ 522 2000
🚌 Cross-city buses

MESPIL HOTEL

mespilhotel.com

With a quiet location on the Grand Canal, and a short walk to the city center, this efficient and modern 260-room hotel has a great selection of spacious family rooms, some sleeping up to five guests.

➕ J9 ✉ 50–60 Mespil Road ☎ 488 4600 🚉 Grand Canal Dock 🚌 10

MOLESWORTH COURT SUITES

molesworthcourt.ie

These contemporary suites and penthouses, located on a quiet street near Grafton Street, have well-equipped kitchens and a living room. Its largest bedrooms sleep six.

➕ H8 ✉ Schoolhouse Lane, off Molesworth Street ☎ 676 4799 🚉 Pearse 🚌 Cross-city buses

THE MORGAN

themorgan.com

Spacious bathrooms and excellent in-room facilities are the hallmarks of this luxurious boutique hotel. The bar overlooks the popular Temple Bar street. Guests can enjoy free use of a nearby gym and pool.

➕ H6 ✉ 10 Fleet Street, Temple Bar ☎ 643 7000 🚉 Tara Street 🚌 Cross-city buses

NUMBER 31

number31.ie

A superb boutique hotel tucked away on a mews lane, Number 31 features a sunken seating area in front of the fireplace and a peaceful walled garden. The rooms combine many Georgian features with funky, modernist style. Guests can expect an excellent breakfast here.

➕ J9 ✉ 31 Leeson Close ☎ 676 5011 🚌 Cross-city buses

GOLF HOTELS

Ireland's reputation as a world-class golfing destination is undisputed, and there are some excellent hotels with great courses just outside Dublin. Try the Portmarnock Hotel and Golf Links, renowned for comfort, good food and world-class golf. The hotel's 18-hole course was designed by Bernard Langer. Conveniently close to the airport.

➕ Off map ✉ Strand Road, Portmarnock ☎ 846 0611; portmarnock.com

For another golf hotel option, see the opposite page for the Deer Park Hotel.

THE SCHOOLHOUSE HOTEL

schoolhousehotel.com

The result of an excellent conversion from a mid 19th-century school, this boutique hotel has 31 rooms, each tastefully designed and dedicated to a prominent name in Irish history. It has an excellent restaurant and bar.

➕ K8 ✉ 2–8 Northumberland Road ☎ 667 5014 🚉 Grand Canal Dock 🚌 Cross-city buses

STAUNTONS ON THE GREEN

stauntonsonthegreen.ie

Many prominent names have lived in this Georgian town house, including poets, politicians and priests. A Dublin favorite, it has 30 spacious guest rooms and a tucked-away, picturesque garden.

➕ H8 ✉ 83 St. Stephen's Green ☎ 478 2300 🚉 Pearse 🚌 Cross-city buses

WYNN'S HOTEL

wynnshotel.ie

Housed in a listed building in north Dublin, Wynn's has a long history and literary connections. The guest rooms are elegant and simple.

➕ H6 ✉ 35–39 Lower Abbey Street ☎ 874 5131 🚌 Cross-city buses; Luas Abbey Street

Luxury Hotels

CLARENCE

theclarence.ie

The chic, modern hotel has 50 boutique rooms, some with river views and balconies, and there is a duplex penthouse. The Octagon Bar has art deco features.

 G7 ✉ 6–8 Wellington Quay ☎ 407 0800 🚇 Tara Street 🚌 Cross-city buses

DYLAN

dylan.ie

This luxury boutique hotel in a former nurses home has 72 glamorous rooms and suites, a smart restaurant and bars.

K9 ✉ Eastmoreland Place ☎ 660 3000 🚌 10

FITZWILLIAM HOTEL

fitzwilliamhoteldublin.com

Some of the 139 bedrooms at this boutique-style hotel overlook a rooftop garden. There's a library and spa plus the renowned Glovers Alley restaurant.

H8 ✉ St. Stephen's Green ☎ 478 7000 🚇 Pearse 🚌 Cross-city buses

GRESHAM

gresham-hotels.com

The 288 elegant bedrooms partner traditional style with modern comfort. It offers several bars and lounges, the Gallery restaurant and use of a nearby gym.

H5 ✉ 23 O'Connell Street Upper ☎ 874 6881 🚇 Connolly 🚌 Cross-city buses

THE MARKER HOTEL

themarkerhoteldublin.com

Striking and contemporary in the regenerated Docklands, the Marker Hotel has spacious, unfussy bedrooms in bold color schemes. An infinity pool, a luxury spa and rooftop dining are glamorous extras.

K7 ✉ Grand Canal Square, Docklands ☎ 687 5100 🚇 Pearse 🚌 Cross-city buses

MERRION

merrionhotel.com

Originally four Georgian houses, the Merrion has 142 luxurious bedrooms that exude period charm. Guests can enjoy the gym, pool and spa, as well as business facilities.

J8 ✉ Merrion Street Upper ☎ 603 0600 🚇 Pearse 🚌 Cross-city buses

THE MORRISON

morrisonhotel.ie

A modern designer heaven, with an urban chic style, the Morrison offers 145 rooms, suites and studios, including the Penthouse Suite. There's a restaurant and a popular cocktail bar.

G6 ✉ Ormond Quay Lower ☎ 887 4200 🚌 Cross-city buses

THE SHELBOURNE

theshelbourne.com

The illustrious Shelbourne Hotel, built in 1824 with a Victorian facade, boasts 265 luxurious rooms with antiques, chandeliers and open fires. Try the excellent food in the Saddle Room, and the intimate 1824 Bar.

H8 ✉ 27 St. Stephen's Green ☎ 663 4500 🚇 Pearse 🚌 Cross-city buses

WESTBURY

doylecollection.com

Tucked away off Grafton Street, this elegant hotel with light-filled rooms and restaurants is a Dublin institution.

H7 ✉ Balfe Street ☎ 679 1122 🚇 Pearse 🚌 Cross-city buses

Dublin is a compact city and is easy to get around on foot. Additionally, buses are numerous and frequent, and the DART is great to use for a trip outside the city.

Planning Ahead

When to Go

Most visitors come between March and October, when the weather is at its best and there is a wider choice of activities. A few attractions are closed in the winter. Dublin is temperate year-round, but be prepared for frequent rain.

AVERAGE DAILY MAXIMUM TEMPERATURES

JAN	FEB	MAR	APR	MAY	JUN	JUL	AUG	SEP	OCT	NOV	DEC
46°F	46°F	50°F	55°F	59°F	64°F	68°F	66°F	63°F	57°F	50°F	46°F
8°C	8°C	10°C	13°C	15°C	18°C	20°C	19°C	17°C	14°C	10°C	8°C

Spring (March to May) is mild with mostly clear skies and a mix of sunshine and showers. April and May are the driest months.

Summer (June to August) is bright and warm but notoriously unpredictable. July is particularly showery. Heat waves are rare.

Autumn (September to November) often has very heavy rain and is mostly overcast, although still quite mild. Even October can be summery.

Winter (December to February) is not usually severe and tends to be wet rather than snowy. Temperatures rarely fall below freezing.

WHAT'S ON

January TradFest Temple Bar.

February/March Dublin International Film Festival.

February/March Six Nations Rugby at Aviva Stadium.

March St. Patrick's Day Festival (several days around 17 Mar).

May Dublin Dance Festival. Docklands Summer Festival. International Dublin Gay Theatre Festival.

June Taste of Dublin food festival, Iveagh Gardens. Bloomsday (16 Jun): celebration of James Joyce's Ulysses. Pride: week-long LGBTQ+ festival.

June–August Music recitals and festivals in parks.

July Dublin Horse Show (RDS)

Late August/early September Liffey Swim (1.5 mile race for men and women).

All-Ireland Hurling and Gaelic Football Finals at Croke Park. Dublin Fringe Festival. Irish Champions Weekend— Leopardstown.

September/October Dublin Theatre Festival.

October Dublin Marathon. Samhain Festival: Halloween parade, fireworks (31 Oct).

Bram Stoker Festival.

December Contemporary Crafts and Design Fair (RDS). Christmas carols and concerts: in churches around the city.

New Year's Eve festival, including fireworks and ringing bells at midnight at Christ Church Cathedral.

Listings

Daily newspapers cover what's on in Dublin.

Dublin online

visitdublin.com
The local tourist board site unveils every aspect of the city. You'll find up-to-date information on accommodations (reserve online), restaurants, entertainment, shopping, nightlife and attractions, as well as insider guides and downloadable city walking tours.

irishtimes.com
Website of the influential *Irish Times*, one of Dublin's daily newspapers. Read up on the news, weather, culture and what's on.

dublincity.ie
This is the official website of Dublin City Council. Look here for details of upcoming events, cultural highlights, plus specific information for day-to-day living and working in the city.

dublinevents.com
A comprehensive guide about upcoming events at venues across Dublin, from theater and cinema to live music, comedy, traditional Irish shows, exhibitions and sports. Plus hotels, restaurants bars and clubs.

entertainment.ie
Decent guide to all events throughout Ireland, with listings of events, festivals, music, theater and cinema.

heritageireland.ie
Useful in-depth information about historical sites and gardens throughout Ireland, including a comprehensive section on Dublin.

ireland.com
Tourism Ireland's site carries a wealth of information on the whole of Ireland, with sections on history, culture, events, activities and gastronomy, plus practical tips. It is a great resource for booking travel and accommodations.

TRAVEL SITES

fodors.com
A complete travel-planning site. You can research prices; book air tickets, cars and rooms; ask questions (and get answers) from fellow travelers; and search travel tips for Dublin and other Irish destinations.

dublinbus.ie
Everything you need to know about the public bus service, including how to buy the best tickets for your needs. Also information about the DART system and the Luas trams.

irishrail.ie
An online timetable and booking site for trains throughout Ireland, including to Belfast.

USING WIFI

All hotels and guesthouses in Dublin have free WiFi for guests. Most restaurants, cafés and bars will also have a WiFi connection— just ask for their login details. All Dublin buses, including the airport bus, display their connection details at the front of the bus.

Getting There

ENTRY REQUIREMENTS

Ireland is a member of the European Union (EU). For the most up-to-date passport and visa information visit the Embassy of Ireland Great Britain website (embassyofireland.co.uk) or Embassy of Ireland USA (embassyofireland.org).

CUSTOMS

The limits for non-EU visitors are 200 cigarettes or 50 cigars or 250g of tobacco; 1 liter of spirits (over 22 percent) or 2 liters of fortified wine, 4 liters of still wine; 50g of perfume. Visitors under 18 are not entitled to the tobacco and alcohol allowances. The guidelines for EU residents (for personal use) are 800 cigarettes, 200 cigars, 1kg of tobacco; 10 liters of spirits (over 22 percent), 20 liters of aperitifs, 90 liters of wine, of which 60 can be sparkling wine, 110 liters of beer.

AIRPORTS

Dublin Airport is 11km (7 miles) north of the city. It is one of the busiest airports in Europe for international passenger traffic, serving over 180 routes to the UK and continental Europe, US, Canada, North Africa and the Middle East, with some 41 airlines. Aer Lingus is the national carrier.

ARRIVING BY AIR

Transportation from Dublin Airport (tel 01 814 1111, dublinairport.com) is straightforward. Airlink Express 747 and 757 buses run between the airport and the main city rail and bus stations. The journey takes 20–30 minutes (longer during morning rush hour) and costs €7 one-way, €12 return (online fares €1 cheaper). Aircoach is a 24-hour coach service serving central Dublin and the main hotels in Ballsbridge/Donnybrook and Leopardstown/Sandyford. Fares range from €6 to €9. Services also to Belfast and Cork. Taxis are metered, and a journey to central Dublin should cost around €30, depending on traffic (but check first). Find car rental companies in the arrivals area.

ARRIVING BY BOAT

Ferries from Holyhead and Liverpool sail into the port of Dublin throughout the year. The ferry journey from Holyhead takes around 3 hours 15 minutes on a traditional ferry or 1 hour 50 minutes via the high-speed options. The journey time between Liverpool and Dublin is approximately 8 hours. Taxis and buses

operate from the port into the city. From Dublin Port take Alexander Road west, turn left to the 3Arena and follow "city centre" signs.

ARRIVING BY TRAIN
There are two main line train stations in Dublin. Passengers from the north of Ireland arrive at Connolly Station, while trains arriving from the south and west operate in and out of Heuston Station. Buses, taxis and Luas trams are available at Connolly and Heuston stations. Heuston also has a DART stop. Call Irish Rail on 01 836 6222 or irishrail.ie.

ARRIVING BY CAR
Traffic drives on the left. Congestion in Dublin is notorious, and on-street parking is expensive and limited. There are multistory car parks in the city hub. The one-way traffic systems can be confusing. Avoid rush hours (morning and evening), keep out of bus lanes and use designated parking areas. Penalties for illegal parking are severe. Check whether your hotel or guesthouse has parking for guests. Always lock your car and keep belongings out of sight.

BREXIT
UK visitors should check the very latest entry requirements as a result of the country's decision to leave the EU. Check if a visa is required along with a valid passport and if reduced-cost medical treatment with the European Health Insurance Card (EHIC) is still available. For more information, visit gov.uk/visit-europe-brexit.

Getting Around

VISITORS WITH DISABILITIES

Access for wheelchair users has improved greatly in Dublin over recent years. Most public buildings and visitor attractions have ramps and elevators. Those with particularly good facilities are the Guinness Storehouse and the Chester Beatty Library. However, it is advisable to check in advance. Dublin buses have incorporated accessible features into their vehicles and many of their routes are wheelchair accessible (☎ 01 703 3024). The Irish Wheelchair Association (☎ 01 818 6455; iwa.ie) can give advice on accessible accommodations, restaurants and pubs in the city. It can also provide information on wheelchair and car rental.

TAXIS

● Useful numbers:

Taxis NRC
☎ 01 677 2222; nrc.ie
Blue Cabs
☎ 01 802 2222;
bluecabs.ie
Ask your hotel or the restaurant to call you a cab.

PUBLIC TRANSPORTATION

The bus number and destination (in English and Irish) are displayed on the front. *An Lar* means city center. Buy tickets on the bus (exact change needed) or before boarding from Dublin Bus office or some newsstands; timetables are also available here. Busáras, the main bus terminus, is north of the River Liffey on Amiens Street.

The DART is a light rail service running from Malahide or Howth in the north of the city to Greystones in the south (irishrail.ie). The main city stations are Connolly (north side) and Pearse (south side). Trains run at least every 5 minutes at peak times, otherwise every 15 minutes Mon–Sat 6.30am–11.30pm and less frequently Sun, 9.30am–11pm. Buy tickets at the station.

The Luas is a tram system operating between the suburbs and central Dublin (luas.ie).

Taxis are in short supply, especially at night. Taxi stands are found outside hotels, train and bus stations, and at busy locations such as St. Stephen's Green and O'Connell Street.

● Dublin Bus (Bus Átha Cliath) operates Mon–Sat 5am–11.30pm, Sun 8am–11.30pm. Check routes (tel 873 4222, dublinbus.ie).
● Nitelink operates Fri–Sat to the suburbs. Buses leave on the hour from D'Olier Street and Westmoreland Street from around midnight to 4am; check for individual routes.
● Bus Éireann Expressway operates a nationwide coach service between Dublin and cities in Ireland (tel 01 836 6111, buseireann.ie).

TRAVEL PASSES

● The Leap Card, an electronic top-up card for Dublin buses, can be bought for a €5 returnable deposit, topped up with credit. They are not valid for ferry services or tours. Fares cost around 20 per cent less than cash tickets.
● You can buy all travel passes from Dublin Bus at 55 Upper O'Connell Street. Selected newsstands sell a limited number of passes.

Essential Facts

ELECTRICITY
- 220V AC. Most hotels have 110V shaver outlets.
- Plugs have three square pins.

EMBASSIES
- Australia: 47-49 St. Stephen's Green, Dublin 2, tel 664 5300, ireland.embassy.gov.au
- Belgium: 1 Elgin Road, Dublin 4, tel 631 5284-86, ireland.diplomatie.belgium.be
- Canada: 7–8 Wilton Terrace, Dublin 2, tel 234 4000, canadainternational.gc.ca/ireland-irlande
- France: 66 Fitzwilliam Lane, Dublin 2, tel 277 5000, ambafrance-ie.org
- Germany: 31 Trimleston Avenue, Booterstown, County Dublin, tel 277 6100, dublin.diplo.de
- Italy: 63–65 Northumberland Road, Dublin 4, tel 660 1744, ambdublino.esteri.it
- Netherlands: 160 Merrion Road, Dublin 4, tel 269 3444, nederlandwereldwijd.nl
- Spain: 17a Merlyn Park, Dublin 4, tel 269 1640/2597, exteriores.gob.es
- United Kingdom: 29 Merrion Road, Dublin 4, tel 205 3700, gov.uk/world/ireland
- U.S. 42 Elgin Road, Ballsbridge, Dublin 4, tel 668 8777, ie.usembassy.gov

EMERGENCY PHONE NUMBERS
- For Police (*garda*), fire and ambulance call 999 (free of charge).

ETIQUETTE
- Dubliners are gregarious, so do not be perturbed if strangers strike up a conversation. However some topics remain sensitive, such as religion or politics.
- Locals can be quite laid-back about time-keeping for social events. If you are invited to someone's home for dinner, aim to arrive there about 10 minutes after the arranged time.
- Groups of friends and acquaintances usually buy drinks in rounds and if you join them, you will be expected to participate.

TOURIST INFORMATION

Tourist offices:
- ✉ Dublin Airport
- ✉ 25 Suffolk Street
- ✉ 14 Upper O'Connell Street
- ✉ County Hall, Marine Road, Dun Laoghaire

All tourist offices are walk-in only. For informaton telephone ☎ 1890 324 583 (in Ireland) or visitdublin.com.

OPENING HOURS

Museums and sights: Most open seven days a week, but some close on Monday, with shorter hours on Sunday. Call for details.
Shops: Open six days a week, some seven days; late-night shopping on Thursday. Supermarkets are open longer hours Wed–Fri. Large suburban shopping malls open Sunday 12–6.
Banks: Mon, Tue, Fri 10–4, Wed 10.30–4, Thu 10–5.

TIPPING

● Tips are not expected in cinemas, gas stations, or in pubs, unless there is table service.

● Ten percent is usual for hairdressers and cab drivers; €2 for porters, and cloakroom attendants. See panel, ▷ 85 for restaurant tipping.

MONEY

The euro has been the official currency of Ireland since 2002. Bank notes are in denominations of €5, €10, €20, €50, €100 and €200, and coins in denominations of 5, 10, 20 and 50 cents and €1 and €2 (1 and 2 cent coins are being phased out).

LGBTQ+ TRAVELERS

● *GCN (Gay Community News)* is a free monthly magazine and is available in bars, clubs and bookshops (gcn.ie) throughout the city.

● LGBT events in Dublin include the *International Dublin Gay Theater Festival* (May), *Pride* (late June) and the *Lesbian and Gay Film Festival* (late July/August).

● For information and advice, contact: Gay Switchboard Dublin (tel 872 1055, https://gcn.ie, open Mon–Fri 6.30pm–9pm, Sat 2–6, Sun 4–6); Outhouse LGBT (105 Capel Street, tel 873 4999, outhouse.ie).

MEDICINES AND MEDICAL TREATMENT

● Ambulance: tel 999 or 112.

● Hospital with 24-hour emergency service: St. James's Hospital (James's Street, Dublin 8; tel 410 3000).

● Dental: emergency treatment (daytimes only): Dublin Dental University Hospital (Lincoln Place; tel 612 7391).

● Minor ailments can usually be treated at pharmacies, but only a limited range of medication can be dispensed without a prescription.

● Pharmacies in Dublin that are open late: Hickey's Pharmacy (55 Lower O'Connell Street, tel 873 0427), City Pharmacy (14 Dame Street, 670 4523).

MONEY MATTERS

● Banks may offer better exchange rates than shops, hotels and bureaux de change.

● The Bureaux de Change at Dublin airport has longer opening hours but charges above-average commission.

● Credit and debit cards can be used in most hotels, shops and restaurants and to withdraw cash from ATMs.

● Currency cards, which you top-up online, can be used to withdraw cash or used as a debit card, and generally attract little or no commission.

NEWSPAPERS AND MAGAZINES

● The daily broadsheets, the *Irish Times* and the *Irish Independent*, are printed in Dublin. The local *Evening Herald* is on sale Mon–Fri at midday. The major UK tabloids also produce separate Irish editions.
● International magazines and newspapers are sold in major bookstores including Eason (40–42 Lower O'Connell Street).
● For events and entertainment listings, see magazines *In Dublin* and *Totally Dublin*.
● *Hot Press* (hotpress.com) is Ireland's music magazine and *Image* (image.ie) is a popular women's magazine. UK magazines are also widely available.

ORGANIZED TOURS

● Dublin Bus Tour is a hop-on, hop-off sightseeing tour. Buy tickets on board the buses, online or at Dublin Tourism in Suffolk Street.
● The Dublin Literary Pub Crawl (dublinpubcrawl.com) is a walking tour that visits pubs frequented by historic literary giants. Guides add to the atmosphere by giving readings from famous Irish tomes. The tour starts from upstairs at the Duke pub, 9 Duke Street (tel 670 5602; runs Apr–Oct nightly 7.30pm; Nov–Mar Thu–Sun 7.30pm).
● The Musical Pub Crawl (musicalpubcrawl. com) starts from the Oliver St. John Gogarty pub (tel 475 3313; runs Apr–Oct nightly 7.30pm; Nov–Mar Thu–Sat 7.30pm). The early pub crawl (7.15pm, Flanagans Bar, O'Connell Street) includes dinner and Irish dancing.
● Take a sightseeing boat cruise with Dublin Discovered (dublindiscovered.ie) and learn about Dublin's history (tel 473 0000; sailings depart from Batchelor's Walk, daily from 10.30am, Mar–Nov).

POST OFFICES

● The main post office, GPO, in O'Connell Street (tel 705 7600) is open Mon–Sat 8.30–6. Other post offices are generally open Mon–Fri 9–5.30, and certain city branches also open

NATIONAL HOLIDAYS

● 1 January; 17 March (St. Patrick's Day); Easter Monday; first Monday in May, June and August; last Monday in October (Samhain); 25 and 26 December.
● Many businesses close on Good Friday.

TOILETS

● Dublin is not noted for its public toilets: use the facilities at a pub, café, shopping mall or large store but, if you do so, it is polite to make a purchase.
● Signs may be in Irish: *mná*: women, *fir*: men.

NEED TO KNOW ESSENTIAL FACTS

LOST PROPERTY

Report loss or theft of a passport to the police immediately. Your embassy or consulate can provide further assistance.

Airport ☎ 814 5555
Ferry port ☎ 607 5519
Train ☎ 703 3299 (Heuston), 703 2358 (Connolly)
Dublin Bus ☎ 703 1321
Bus Éireann ☎ 836 6111

STUDENTS

● Dublin is very student-friendly.
● An International Student Identity Card (ISIC) secures discounts in many cinemas, theaters, shops, restaurants and attractions.
● Discounts may be available on travel cards for the bus and DART.

on Saturday. Some suburban offices may close at lunchtime.
● Stamps are sold at post offices, some newsstands, hotels and shops. Stamps are also available from coin-operated machines.
● Postboxes are green.

SENSIBLE PRECAUTIONS

● Be cautious and keep valuables out of sight.
● Don't leave bags on the backs of chairs.
● Make a separate note of all passport, ticket and credit card numbers.
● Avoid Phoenix Park at night.
● After dark, women should sit downstairs on buses, or in a busy car on trains. Take a taxi rather than a late-night bus out to the suburbs.

TELEPHONES

● Public telephones use coins or phone cards (sold in post offices and newsagents).
● For the operator, dial 10; for directory enquiries dial 11850, 11890 or 11811.
● Calls from hotels are expensive. Look for public phones on streets, in pubs and shopping malls. Make the most of free WiFi in hotels, restaurants, etc, to make international calls from your smartphone with Whatsapp or Viber.
● For a longer stay, buy a local SIM card for your mobile phone if it is unlocked.
● When calling Ireland from the UK dial 00 353. The code for Dublin is 01 (omit the zero when calling from abroad).
● To call the UK from Dublin, dial 00 44.
● When calling from the US dial 011 353. The code for Dublin is 01 (omit the zero when calling from abroad).
● To call the US from Dublin, dial 00 1.

TV AND RADIO

● Radio Telefis Éireann (RTÉ) is the state broadcasting authority. It has four FM radio stations and five digital radio stations. Its television stations are RTÉ 1, RTÉ 2 and RTÉ News Now.
● TG4 is the National Irish Language station. TV3 Ireland is independent.

Language

Irish is the official first language of the Republic of Ireland with English, although English is the spoken language in Dublin. It is uncommon to hear Irish spoken in Dublin, but the language is enjoying a revival and is fashionable among a younger set proud of their cultural traditions. It is an important symbol of national identity. You will come across Irish on signposts, buses, trains and official documents, and the news (*an nuacht*) is broadcast *as gaeilge* on television and radio. Telefis Na Gaeilge's *TG4* is a dedicated Irish-language channel with English subtitles. The areas known as the Gaeltacht are pockets of the country where Irish is the main tongue and you will find maps and signposts using only Gaelic. These areas are mainly on the western side of Ireland. The Irish language is difficult for the beginner to grasp, with words often pronounced quite differently from the way they are written. Also, there are different Irish dialects and spellings in different regions.

SOME IRISH WORDS TO LOOK OUT FOR

An Lar	City center	*Leitris*	Toilet
Baile Átha Cliath	Dublin	*Mná*	Ladies
Céilí	Dance	*Fir*	Gents
Craic	Good time	*Le do thoil*	Please
Dia dhuit	Hello	*Níl/ní hea*	No
Dúnta	Closed	*Oifig an phoist*	Post Office
Fáilte	Welcome	*Oscailte*	Open
Gardaí	Police	*Slán*	Goodbye
Go raibh maith aguth	Thank you	*Sláinte*	Cheers
		Tá/sea	Yes

PLACE NAMES AND THEIR IRISH ROOT

IRISH ROOT	MEANING	IRISH PLACE NAMES
ar, ard	height	Ardmore, Ardgroom
áth, atha	ford	Athlone, Athy
bal, baile, ballya	town	Ballyhack
beg, beag	small	Beaghmore Stone Circles, Lough Beg
cashel	castle	Rock of Cashel
drom, drum	a ridge	Drombeg Stone Circle, Drumsna
dun, dún	a fort	Dundalk, Dún Laoghaire
innis, ennis	island	Enniskerry, Enniscorthy
kil, kill, cil	a church	Killarney, Glencolumbkille
knock, cnoc	a hill	Knocknarea Mountain, Knockferry
lis, liss, lios	a ring fort	Listowel, Lisdoonvarna
mor, mór	big or great	Aranmore, Lismore
rath	a ring fort	Rathfarnham, Rathdrum
slieve	a mountain	Slieve Bloom, Slieve League

Timeline

BEFORE AD 1000

The Celts landed in Ireland in the 4th century BC and their influence remains even today. Their religious rites included complex burial services.

Archeological excavations have produced some magnificent gold pieces and jewelry, some of which can be seen in the National Museum (▷ 68).

According to legend, St. Patrick converted many of Dublin's inhabitants to Christianity in the fifth century AD. In AD841 Vikings established a trading station, probably near present-day Kilmainham. The Vikings later moved downstream, to the area around Dublin Castle, in the 10th century.

1825 High King Brian Boru defeats the Dublin Vikings.

1172 After Norman barons invade Ireland from Wales, King Henry II gives Dublin to the men of Bristol.

1348–51 The Black Death claims one third of Dublin's inhabitants.

1592 Queen Elizabeth I grants a charter for the founding of Trinity College.

1700s Dublin's population expands from 40,000 to 172,000.

1713 Jonathan Swift is appointed Dean of St. Patrick's Cathedral.

1714 Start of the Georgian era, Dublin's great period of classical architecture.

1745 The building of Leinster House (now home of the Irish Parliament) leads to new housing south of the river.

1759 The Guinness Brewery is founded.

1782 The Irish Parliament secures legislative independence from Britain.

1800 The Act of Union is passed and the Irish Parliament abolishes itself.

1845 The start of Ireland's Great Famine.

1916 The Easter Rising.

1919 First session of Dáil Éireann (the Irish Parliament) in Mansion House.

1922 Civil War declared. After 718 years in residence, British forces evacuate Dublin Castle.

1963 Visit by President John F. Kennedy.

1979 The Pope says mass in Phoenix Park to more than 1.3 million people.

1990 Mary Robinson is elected president—Ireland's first female president.

1997 Divorce becomes legal under certain circumstances.

1998 The Good Friday Agreement sees a ceasefire in Northern Ireland.

2001 IRA is decommissioned in December.

2011 Queen Elizabeth II is the first British monarch to visit Ireland since its independence.

2013 Legislation is passed allowing abortion in certain circumstances.

2015 A referendum results in Ireland legalizing same-sex marriage.

2020 Ireland awaits confirmation of issues resulting from the UK's exit from the EU.

EASTER RISING

With the founding of the Gaelic League in 1893 and the Abbey Theatre in 1904, the movement for independence gathered momentum in Ireland. Republicans capitalized on England's preoccupation with World War I to stage a rising in 1916 and declare an independent Republic in Dublin's General Post Office. It was doomed to failure but the execution of several of the insurrection's leaders made rebels out of many Irish royalists, leading five years later to the creation of an Irish Free State. The Anglo-Irish Treaty was signed in 1921, followed by a Civil War in 1922, lasting 22 months. In 1936 the Free State became known as Eire under a new Constitution. The Republic finally became a reality in 1949.

From far left: An early city map; helmets in St. Patrick's Cathedral; Great Courtyard of Dublin Castle; Queen Victoria visits Dublin (1900)

Index

Dublin 25 Best

WRITTEN BY Dr. Peter Harbison, Melanie Morris, Hilary Weston and Jackie Staddon
UPDATED BY Emma Levine
SERIES EDITOR Clare Ashton
COVER DESIGN Jessica Gonzalez
DESIGN WORK Liz Baldin
IMAGE RETOUCHING AND REPRO Ian Little

© AA Media Limited 2021 (registered office: Grove House, Lutyens Close, Basingstoke, RG24 8AG, registered number 06112600).

All rights reserved. Published in the United States by MH Sub I, LLC dba Fodor's Travel. No maps, illustrations, or other portions of this book may be reproduced in any form without written permission from the publisher.

Fodor's is a registered trademark of MH Sub I, LLC.

Published in the UK by AA Media Limited.

ISBN 978-1-64097-340-4

NINTH EDITION

All details in this book are based on information supplied to us at press time. Always confirm information when it matters, especially if you're making a detour to visit a specific place. Fodor's expressly disclaims any liability, loss, or risk, personal or otherwise, that is incurred as a consequence of the use of any of the contents of this book.

Printed and bound in China by 1010 Printing Group Limited.

10 9 8 7 6 5 4 3 2 1

A05743
Maps in this title based on Ordnance Survey Ireland.
Permit No. 9226 © Ordnance Survey Ireland/Government of Ireland and on data available from openstreetmap.org © under the Open Database License found at opendatacommons.org
Transport map © Communicarta Ltd, UK

We would like to thank the following photographers, companies and picture libraries for their assistance in the preparation of this book.

2–4t AA/S Day; 4l AA/S Whitehorne; 5t AA/S Day; 5c Michele Oenbrink / Alamy Stock Photo; 6t AA/S Day; 6cl AA/C Coe; 6c AA/Slidefile; 6cr AA/M Short; 6b AA/S McBride; 7t AA/S Day; 7cl AA/L Blake; 7cr AA/S Day; 7bl AA/S Day; 7br Ireland's Content Pool/ Tony Pleavin; 8t AA/S Day; 9t AA/S Day; 10t AA/S Day; 10ctr AA/S Whitehorne; 10cr AA/S Day; 10cbr Ireland's Content Pool/Tourism Ireland; 11t AA/S Day; 11ctl Ireland's Content Pool/Jonathon Hessian; 11cl–11cbl Ireland's Content Pool; 12 AA/S Day; 13t AA/S Day; 13ctl AA/Slidefile; 13cl Ireland's Content Pool/Rob Durston Photography; 13cbl AA/ Slidefile; 13bl Ireland's Content Pool/Tony Pleavin; 14t AA/S Day; 14ctr AA/S McBride; 14cr AA/S Day; 14cbr Ireland's Content Pool/Tourism Ireland; 14br AA/S Whitehorne; 15 AA/S Day; 16t AA/S Day; 16tr Hemis / Alamy Stock Photo; 16cr Patrick Guilbaud; 16br Dublin Zoo; 17t AA/S Day; 17tl AA/M Short; 17ctl Buswell's Hotel, Dublin; 17c Photodisc; 17cbl Ireland's Content Pool/DRTA; 17bl Dublinia; 18t AA/S Day; 18tr AA/S Day; 18ctr Ireland's Content Pool/Tourism Ireland; 18cbr AA/Slidefile; 18br Ireland's Content Pool; 19b AA/S Day; 20 AA/S Day; 24l © The Trustees of the Chester Beatty Library, Dublin; 24r © The Trustees of the Chester Beatty Library, Dublin; 25l AA/S Day; 25r–26 Ireland's Content Pool/Rob Durston Photographer; 27tl AA/S Day; 27tr AA/S Day; 27cl Ireland's Content Pool/Rob Durston Photographer; 27cr AA/S Day; 28, 29t, 29cl, 29cr Dublinia Ltd; 30t Ireland's Content Pool/Rob Durston Photographer; 30c–30/31 Courtesy of Guinness Storehouse; 32l Ireland's Content Pool/Rob Durston Photographer; 32r Ireland's Content Pool/davisonphoto.com; 33l AA/S Day; 33r AA/C Coe; 34t AA/Slidefile; 35t AA/Slidefile; 36 Ireland's Content Pool/Jonathan Hession; 37 AA/S Whitehorne; 38 AA/S Whitehorne; 39 AA/Slidefile; 40t AA/Slidefile; 41t AA/Slidefile; 41c Ireland's Content Pool/Rob Durston Photographer; 42t Ireland's Content Pool/Rob Durston Photography; 43t Ireland's Content Pool/Rob Durston Photography; 44t Rob Durston Photography; 45 Hon Lau - Dublin/Alamy Stock Photo; 48l Collection & image © Hugh Lane Gallery, Dublin (Reg. No. 1442); 48r Collection & image © Hugh Lane Gallery, Dublin (Reg. No. 1442)/Ireland's Content Pool; 49l AA/S Day; 49c Ireland's Content Pool/DRTA; 49r AA/M Short; 50/1 Ireland's Content Pool/Epic Ireland Property; 51tr Epic Ireland; 51cr Epic Ireland; 52l Ireland's Content Pool; 52r Ireland's Content Pool; 53l Killian Broderick/James Joyce Centre; 53c AA/S Day; 53r Ireland's Content Pool/Brian Morrison; 54l, 54r Jameson Distillery Bow Street; 55 National Museum of Decorative Arts; 56t AA/Slidefile; 56bl 14 Henrietta Street/Marc O'Sullivan; 56br AA/Slidefile; 57t AA/Slidefile; 58t Ireland's Content Pool/Jonathan Hession; 59t Ireland's Content Pool/Clara Hooper; 60t DigitalVision; 61t DigitalVision; 61c AA/S McBride; 62t AA/S McBride; 63 Ireland's Content Pool/Brian Morrison; 66l, 66r Little Museum of Dublin; 67l, 67r MoLI Museum; 68l © Fennell Photography; 68r © NGI Photographer Roy Hewson; 69l AA/S Day; 69r Ireland's Content Pool/Rob Durston Photography; 70tl Ireland's Content Pool/Tony Pearson; 70cl Ireland's Content Pool/Niamh Fahy; 71 Ireland's Content Pool/ Niamh Fahy; 72t Ireland's Content Pool/Brian Morrison; 72c Ireland's Content Pool/Brian Morrison; 72/3 AA/S McBride; 74t AA/Slidefile; 74b Ireland's Content Pool/Rob Durston Photography; 75t AA/Slidefile; 75b Ireland's Content Pool/Matthew Thompson; 76t AA/ Slidefile; 76bl Ireland's Content Pool; 76br Viking Splash; 77 Ireland's Content Pool/ Jonathan Hession; 78t–81t Ireland's Content Pool/Tourism Ireland; 82t Ireland's Content Pool/Rob Durston Photography; 83t Ireland's Content Pool/Rob Durston Photography; 84t Ireland's Content Pool/Rob Durston Photography; 85c AA/S Day; 85t AA/S Day; 86t AA/S Day; 87t AA/S Day; 88t AA/S Day; 89 AA/C Jones; 92 GAA Museum; 93l Ireland's Content Pool/Peter Moloney; 93r Ireland's Content Pool/Peter Moloney; 94 Courtesy of Irish Museum of Modern Art/Ros Kavanagh; 95 AA/S Whitehorne; 96 The Office of Public Works; 97 Dublin Zoo/Patrick Bolger; 98t AA/Slidefile; 98bl AA/S Whitehorne; 99t AA/Slidefile; 99b AA/SWhitehorne; 100t AA/M Short; 100bl AA/M Short; 100br Ireland's Content Pool; 101t AA/M Short; 101bl AA/S Whitehorne; 102t AA/C Jones; 102bl AA/C Jones; 102br AA/C Jones; 103t AA/C Jones; 103bl AA/Slidefile; 103bc AA/M Short; 103br Ireland's Content Pool; 104t AA/M Short; 104c AA/Slidefile; 105t AA/Slidefile; 106t ImageState; 108t AA/C Sawyer; 108ctr The Morrison Hotel; 108cr AA/C Sawyer; 108cbr Buswell's Hotel, Dublin; 108br The Morrison Hotel; 109t AA/C Sawyer; 110t AA/C Sawyer; 111t AA/C Sawyer; 112t AA/C Sawyer; 114 Ireland's Content Pool; 115 Ireland's Content Pool; 116 Ireland's Content Pool; 117t Ireland'sContent Pool; 117c Irish Ferries; 118t Ireland's Content Pool; 119b Ireland's Content Pool; 120t–124t Ireland's Content Pool; 124bl AA/Slidefile; 124bc AA/S Day; 124/125 AA/Slidefile; 125t Ireland's Content Pool; 125br AA.

Every effort has been made to trace the copyright holders, and we apologise in advance for any accidental errors. We would be happy to apply the corrections in the following edition of this publication.

Titles in the Series